W9-CEV-027

HOW TO

Be a

GENTLEMAN

OTHER GENTLEMANNERS™ BOOKS

A Gentleman Entertains
John Bridges and Bryan Curtis

As a Gentleman Would Say
John Bridges and Bryan Curtis

A Gentleman Gets Dressed Up
John Bridges and Bryan Curtis

A Gentleman Walks Down the Aisle
John Bridges and Bryan Curtis

Toasts and Tributes
John Bridges and Bryan Curtis

50 Things Every Young Gentleman Should Know
John Bridges and Bryan Curtis

How to Be a Lady
Candace Simpson-Giles

As a Lady Would Say
Sheryl Shade

How to Raise a Lady
Kay West

How to Raise a Gentleman
Kay West

50 Things Every Young Lady Should Know
Kay West

A Lady at the Table
Sheryl Shade with John Bridges

A Gentleman at the Table
John Bridges and Bryan Curtis

A Gentleman Abroad
John Bridges and Bryan Curtis

HOW TO
Be a
GENTLEMAN

REVISED AND EXPANDED

••

A CONTEMPORARY GUIDE TO
COMMON COURTESY

JOHN BRIDGES

THOMAS NELSON
Since 1798

NASHVILLE DALLAS MEXICO CITY RIO DE JANEIRO

© 1998, 2008, 2012 by John Bridges

All rights reserved. No portion of this book may be reproduced, stored in a retrieval system, or transmitted in any form or by any means—electronic, mechanical, photocopy, recording, scanning, or other—except for brief quotations in critical reviews or articles, without the prior written permission of the publisher.

Published in Nashville, Tennessee, by Thomas Nelson. Thomas Nelson is a trademark of Thomas Nelson, Inc.

Thomas Nelson, Inc. titles may be purchased in bulk for educational, business, fund-raising, or sales promotional use. For information, please e-mail SpecialMarkets@ThomasNelson.com.

Illustrations by Alicia Adkerson, Adkerson Design

ISBN: 978-1-4016-0473-8 (third edition)

The Library of Congress has cataloged the earlier edition as follows:

Bridges, John, 1950–
How to be a gentleman : a timely guide to timeless manners / John Bridges.—Rev. and expanded.
   p. cm.
 ISBN: 978-1-4016-0335-9 (hardcover)
 ISBN: 978-1-4016-0351-9 (SE)
 1. Etiquette for men. I. Title.
BJ1601.B76 2008
395.1'42—dc22   2007045574

Printed in the United States of America

12 13 14 15 16 WOR 5 4 3 2 1

*For Clay Isaacs, who was born
knowing all these things*
(1998 edition)

*For Bill Walker, who has listened for
25 years' worth of Sundays*
(2008 edition)

CONTENTS

Contents

INTRODUCTION

When the first edition of *How to Be a Gentleman* was published ten years ago, correct, considerate behavior was being challenged on every side. The premise of that book was that men, as a rule, leave it up to the women in their lives (their mothers, their wives, their girlfriends, and women who are simply their friends, with no blood relation and no romantic attachment) to tell them how to behave.

Since it seemed to answer all the burning good-behavior questions of the moment, *How to Be a Gentleman* proved to be hugely successful; in fact, it has gone on to be translated into more than a dozen foreign languages, doing its part to bring civility to the world at large. Nevertheless, life has changed a great deal over the past ten years, and gentlemen are now left on their own, almost at every turn. Cell phones are everywhere, barking out at us in airports, in grocery stores, and in movie theatres. Unless a gentleman is an absolute Luddite, e-mail is a central part of his life. He must remind himself, at all times, to check up on his text messages. Written correspondence seems even more antiquated than before. Dress codes seem to fluctuate every time a new star wears his shirttail out or tucks his shirttail in while walking down a red carpet.

And yet certain truths remain unchanged, and the

desire for gentlemanliness persists, as well. No matter how much the world may change, a gentleman still needs to know how to behave, from day to day and from occasion to occasion. If he drops a fork, he still wants to know whether he should pick it up or leave it lying on the floor.

Married or not, a gentleman will be expected to go to parties and to entertain. He has business associates to deal with and coworkers with whom he must get along. He needs to know how to set a table. He needs to know how to introduce two of his best friends.

And he needs to know how to tie a bow tie, all by himself, at a moment's notice.

Ultimately, however, being a gentleman has little to do with tying a tie or fumbling with the flatware. Instead, it requires only a little logic, a bit of forethought, and a great deal of consideration for others. It is not about complicated rules and convoluted instructions. It is about trying to make life easier for other people. It is about honestly and sincerely being a nice guy.

For a nice guy, the noblest virtues are camaraderie, dependability, and unswerving loyalty. He realizes that it is an oversimplification to suggest that a gentleman's future might be ruined if he were to eat his entrée with a salad fork. That is why this book spells out what a man really needs to know if he plans to make his way in this world. Simply acting like a gentleman is not enough. It is being a gentleman that is important, and that means thinking of others, being there when you are needed, and knowing when you are not needed.

It truly is possible for a man to learn to be a gentleman if he has the direction he needs. For that reason, the women of the world have welcomed this book for over a decade.

They will welcome this new edition now. And gentlemen everywhere will be glad to see it, too, safe in the knowledge that an ever newer world can be an ever nicer world as well.

THE FUNDAMENTAL THINGS APPLY

10 Eternal Truths of the Gentlemanly Life

1. A gentleman says "please" and "thank you," readily and often.
2. A gentleman does not disparage the beliefs of others—whether they relate to matters of faith, politics, or sports teams.
3. A gentleman always carries a handkerchief, and is ready to lend it, especially to a weeping lady, should the need arise.
4. A gentleman never allows a door to slam in the face of another person—male or female, young or old, absolute stranger or longtime best friend.
5. A gentleman does not make jokes about race, religion, gender, or sexual orientation; neither does he find such jokes amusing.
6. A gentleman knows how to stand in line and how to wait his turn.
7. A gentleman is always ready to offer a hearty handshake.

8. A gentleman keeps his leather shoes polished and his fingernails clean.
9. A gentleman admits when he is wrong.
10. A gentleman does not pick a fight.

Chapter One

A GENTLEMAN EXPERIENCES REAL LIFE

A gentleman knows how to make others feel comfortable.

———

If a gentleman has a cold, and especially if he is running a fever, he declines all social invitations. If it is possible, he even stays away from the office.

———

Even if he lives alone, a gentleman never drinks milk directly from the container.

A gentleman knows that unseemly habits, although they may seem innocuous, can easily become hard, or even impossible, to break.

A Gentleman and his
cell phone

Although cell phones have become ubiquitous in the modern world, a gentleman does his best to use his cell phone in the most unobtrusive manner possible. He knows that, while many may consider a cell phone to be a necessity, there is no reason he should be obnoxious when using one. In fact, cell phones, and even wireless headsets, have become so common that no one is likely to be impressed by the fact that a gentleman owns one. He need not flaunt his newest gadgets, no matter how expensive or cutting-edge they may be, in hopes of impressing others with his social or professional status. A gentleman who seeks to shore up his self-image by the use of gadgetry, especially among strangers, is a very needy gentleman indeed.

A gentleman knows that incessant use of his cell phone can only make it clear that he values the person on the other end of the telephone conversation far more highly than the persons who are in his company. Such behavior is, at its best, ill mannered and irritating. At its worst, it grows tedious and may well lead to unpleasant confrontations with total strangers, theater ushers, train conductors, or airport security.

A gentleman's telephone calls—whether they concern business or private matters—are still his personal affair. He does not force others to listen while he negotiates a real estate deal, while he makes plans for a Saturday-night outing, or while he recreates, in vivid detail, every play of the past weekend's rugby game. Other people, after all, are probably no more interested in the dealings of his day-to-day existence than he is interested in theirs.

If a gentleman finds that he truly must initiate, or receive, a phone call while he is in a public place, he moves to the place where he is least likely to become a nuisance to others. He knows that it is virtually impossible to conduct a quiet cell phone conversation—especially when he is in a crowded restaurant, the aisle of a grocery store, or the lobby of a theater. If the person on the other end of the conversation can hear him, a gentleman had best assume that every other person within earshot can probably hear him, too.

Even in a business meeting, or when he is conducting business at mealtime, a gentleman still says, "Excuse me" before answering a call—even if it is related to the business at hand. He does not make phone calls during a business meeting, unless they are pertinent to the topic that is currently on the table and unless it is appropriate for the content of the conversation to be shared with everyone else within hearing distance.

A gentleman would never be so rude, or self-important, as to cover the phone with his hand, turn his head away from the rest of the table, and mutter, "Excuse me, folks, but this isn't something everybody here needs to be in on."

A gentleman knows that it is appropriate for him to use his cell phone . . .

- if he is alone
- if he is certain that his conversation will not disturb or annoy others
- if he is a doctor, receiving a call from his answering service or from his office
- if he is a father, expecting a report from his children or from their babysitter
- if he is at a raucous event such as a football game, where his shouting will only add to the general uproar
- if it is truly necessary for him to bring another person into the conversation at a business meeting, at that very moment
- if he truly believes there is a chance that an emergency is in the offing

A GENTLEMAN EXPERIENCES REAL LIFE

A gentleman does not use his cell phone . . .

- when he is behind the wheel of a vehicle, of any type
- in the midst of a church service or during a theater performance, a movie, or at a concert
- at a table in a restaurant of any type— be it fast food or first class
- in the waiting room, or in the examining room, at a doctor's office
- when standing in line at the grocery store, the post office, a deli, or any other place where customers may find themselves trapped as unwilling witnesses to his conversation
- in an elevator, unless he is alone, or in the company of only friends or coworkers
- in the workout room at his gym
- on the "quiet car" of a train
- in the cabin of an airplane, unless some actual, dire emergency demands it
- in any place where signage, or a public announcement, notifies him that the use of cell phones is not permitted

A gentleman who happens to be a doctor checks his pager with an usher or changes it to the silent setting. However, if he is a real estate agent out for an evening at the theater, he turns off his pager and his cell phone entirely. A real-estate closing is not a life-threatening emergency.

———

A gentleman does not switch on his cell phone and launch into a conversation the moment his plane has landed, simply because a flight attendant has told him it is safe to do so.

———

If a flight attendant tells a gentleman to turn off his cell phone, his MP3 player, his laptop, or any other electronic device, he does so immediately. He does not behave childishly, attempting to stay on the phone until he has been singled out for having ignored the safety instructions.

Although a gentleman may be enjoying music, by means of his personal sound system and with his earbuds plugged in, he still keeps the volume turned to a reasonable level, knowing that an earth-shattering sound level may well be shattering the nerves of the persons seated near him.

———

A gentleman does not assume that, because his wireless headset is inconspicuous, his conversations are inconspicuous, as well.

———

Whenever a gentleman uses his cell phone or his headset on a crowded sidewalk or in the aisle of a grocery store, he still keeps track of where he is going. No matter how important or intriguing his conversation may be, it still does not justify his ramming into another shopper's grocery cart.

A gentleman does not use his camera phone in ways that intrude upon the privacy of others.

———

A gentleman understands that if the taking of photographs is prohibited at any concert or other performance or in an art gallery, that prohibition also includes camera-phone pictures.

———

A gentleman does not attempt to walk and send a text message at the same time.

———

A gentleman does not send text messages, or check for text messages sent to him, during a movie or a live performance of any kind, much less during a worship service. He knows that the glow from his hand-held device, no matter how discreetly he attempts to conceal it, will almost inevitably distract others.

A gentleman understands that, should he elect to send or receive text messages during a performance or a worship service, the people around him may assume that he has little interest in the activities at hand. In more than a few cases, unfortunately, their assumption will be right.

———

A gentleman understands that, for good or ill, as he walks down a sidewalk while engaged in a conversation via his wireless headset, passersby may understandably take him for a paranoid schizophrenic.

A Gentleman Goes to
the Theater

Because he respects other people, a gentleman always shows up on time for any performance, whether it is a concert, a motion picture, or a stage play. If he arrives late, he does not attempt to be seated until there is a suitable break in the performance. (In the case of a play or a musical comedy, his tardiness may require him to wait until intermission.) In every case, he follows the instructions of the ushers. If he behaves himself, a gentleman knows, a kindly usher may quietly slip him into a seat on the back row.

A gentleman never forgets that watching a live performance is not the same thing as watching a TV show in his own living room. He does not talk during the performance—even during the very loudest music or sound effects. He does not shift about in his seat unnecessarily.

If a gentleman has a tendency to cough, he always carries a mint or throat lozenge. Should he find himself surprised by an uncontrollable coughing fit, a gentleman leaves the auditorium—both for his own good and for the good of others.

At a concert or any other musical performance, a gentleman does not applaud until the end of a complete musical number. If he is unsure, he is well advised not to start an ovation alone.

Without even being asked to do so, a gentleman turns off his cell phone, or any other electronic device he is carrying on his person, as soon as he enters the theater. (He also understands that, in this case, "off" means the phone is completely silenced—not simply switched to the "vibrate" mode.) Because he knows others may be wishing to study their program notes or simply to prepare themselves, mentally, for the performance ahead, he does not engage in cell phone chitchat once he has settled into his seat.

When a gentleman makes his way down a row in a crowded theater, he faces the people who are already in their seats. A gentleman never forces others to stare at his backside.

————

A gentleman does not hum along, sing along, or beat time to the rhythm at any concert, unless the performers have invited him and his fellow audience members to do so.

————

If a gentleman has left a telephone message for, or sent an e-mail to, another person, he does not leave badgering follow-up calls or insistent follow-up e-mails, especially if no deadline is involved.

————

A gentleman does not hesitate to screen his calls.

A Gentleman Goes to
a Wedding

Although it is true that any wedding is technically a public event (since it recognizes the legal union of two people), a gentleman only shows up at weddings to which he has been invited. If his invitation does not say "and guest," he attends alone, even if a reception follows. He arrives on time and sits on the appropriate side of the aisle (the left side, if he is a friend of the bride; the right side, if he is a friend of the groom; if he knows them both, he sits on the side with the greater number of empty seats). During the ceremony, he stands when everyone else does, and he does not chat during the music. At the reception he speaks to the bride and groom and to their parents (no matter how many divorces are involved). If there is dancing, he does his part, partnering as many bridesmaids as possible.

If he is not invited to the wedding reception, he is not obligated to give a gift; however, he does not consider it an undue obligation, in any case, to help the couple start out in married life. The gift he sends may be as simple, or as elaborate, as his finances will allow.

A gentleman does not bring his gift with him to the church or to the reception. Instead, he has it sent or he delivers it himself, well ahead of the wedding. If he is unable to send his gift ahead of time—because of his schedule, his financial situation, or his simple forgetfulness—he does not fret about sending it late. He may send a gift at any point during the year following the wedding, knowing that a well-mannered bride and groom will appreciate his thoughtfulness and generosity, at any time.

If he is invited to the reception, a separate reception card will probably be enclosed with the invitation. That card, if it is correctly worded, will indicate whether or not he is expected to wear black tie. If the wedding takes place in a very large church or a hotel ballroom, and if the invitation is an extremely formal one, engraved on heavy stock, he may assume that black tie will be appropriate. If he does not own black tie and does not wish to rent his formalwear, he can always feel at ease wearing his best dark suit, black shoes, and a conservative tie.

If he remains uncertain as to the dress code for the festivities, however, a gentleman goes ahead and contacts the mother of the bride, telling her straight-forwardly, "I'm looking forward to Betsey and Hayworth's wedding on the nineteenth, but I was wondering: Do you think most of the gentlemen will be wearing black tie?"

In no case does a gentleman ever wear black tie before five in the evening, no matter what the invitation requests.

A Gentleman at the Pool

Not every gentleman has a private pool. He may live in an apartment building, in a condominium, or in a subdivision, where any number of people may have the right to share the swimming pool, all at the same time. If all the residents of the building, the condominium, or the subdivision are adults, a gentleman may assume that the accepted rules of poolside behavior will be respected. He does not snatch the last chaise longue, unless he is certain no other sunbather has established ownership of it. Nevertheless, a bath towel, casually slung across a chaise or a pool chair and left lying there for more than forty-five minutes does not establish ownership of that chaise or pool chair, and a gentleman may claim rights of abandonment, simply by asking, "Does anybody know whether somebody is using this chair?" No matter what the response, he may simply fold up the abandoned towel, in a respectful way, and assume ownership of the chaise or chair. If the affronted sunbather returns, a gentleman simply says, "The chaise had been empty for so long, I simply folded your towels and set them here. I hope I kept them in good order."

A gentleman never borrows another person's sunblock—unless it is offered. And he never offers to share his own sunblock or to slather down the back of a fellow sunbather, unless he has been asked to do so.

If unruly children are disrupting the pool, a gentleman may call this behavior to the attention of the children's parents or their temporary overseers. If nothing else seems to work, and if the children are old enough to understand simple English, he may say something frank, such as: "If you're going to splash people in the pool, please go down to the other end and splash people you know. Please do not splash me."

It is astounding the impact such a remark can have on undisciplined children, especially coming from strangers.

A gentleman knows that the gym is
a place for working out, not merely a
place for socializing, and certainly not a
place for finding a new a love interest or
attempting to impress others.

———

In the workout room, a gentleman
does not hog the weights.

———

A gentleman waits his turn before using
the workout machines.

———

A gentleman respects the time limits set
for the use of cardiovascular equipment.

———

In the midst of even his most strenuous
workout, a gentleman does not grunt
more loudly than necessary.

———

If a gentleman tends to have athlete's foot,
he wears shower shoes at the gym.

After he has finished with an exercise machine or with a weight bench, a gentleman wipes it down with a towel and uses a spray-bottle cleaner, if such is provided.

———

A gentleman may do as he pleases in his own shower, but he does not shave in the shower at the gym. He never takes another gentleman's towel.

———

If a gentleman shaves at his health club, he always rinses out the sink.

A Gentleman Attends
a Funeral

A gentleman recognizes that a funeral is a time for paying respects. He wears a dark suit, a white shirt, a somber tie, and a pair of black shoes. If there is a wake, a reception, or a visitation with the family of the deceased, he arrives on time and waits quietly in the receiving line. He keeps his remarks simple, out of respect for the grieving person's overwrought emotions. A statement such as, "I am sorry about your loss, Mrs. Magnuson. Your husband was a wonderful person," is appropriate. During the service, a gentleman does not engage the other mourners in conversation. He sits where the ushers tell him to sit. He always signs the book.

A gentleman may attend the funeral of anyone he has known personally or professionally, at least if they have been on speaking terms. If the deceased person has shown him particular kindness—especially if he has ever been entertained in the deceased person's home—a gentleman makes it a point to pay his respects and offer his condolences.

If the family of the deceased person requests that flowers not be sent, a gentleman does not send them. (He knows that, in Judaism and in some other religious traditions, flowers are never sent to the funeral.) Instead, he makes a contribution to an appropriate charity in the departed person's memory.

A gentleman knows how to behave in other people's houses of worship. If the congregation stands, he stands. He does not, however, have to cross himself, bow, or kneel.

———

If a gentleman attends synagogue and is offered a yarmulke (the traditional head covering worn by men at Conservative and Orthodox Jewish services), he puts it on.

———

A gentleman does not pick his nose in public. Knowing that bad habits are far too easily formed, he is wise if he does not pick his nose in private, either.

———

When a gentleman walks his dog, he assumes responsibility for his pet's poop.

———

If a gentleman is lost, he admits it. He readily asks for directions.

A Gentleman Experiences Real Life

For reasons of courtesy and safety, a gentleman does not dawdle at the automated teller machine. If other people are in line behind him, he does not waste time, checking all his savings account balances. He completes his transaction and moves on.

———————

A gentleman never eats his lunch while he is behind the wheel of a vehicle.

———————

If a gentleman eats in bed, he always changes the sheets.

———————

Even if a gentleman does not eat in bed, he changes his bedsheets at least every two weeks.

———————

When a gentleman is finished with the dryer, he cleans the lint filter.

At the Laundromat, a gentleman only takes another person's laundry out of the washer or the dryer if he is sure the cycle is done. He always treats another person's belongings with the most meticulous care.

———

A gentleman uses his turn signals.

———

A gentleman does not use his car horn indiscriminately. On the other hand, he is not sheepish about giving an occasional honk to avert disaster.

———

A gentleman does not tailgate.

———

A gentleman does not run yellow lights, much less red ones.

A gentleman parks his car carefully. He does not bang his car door into the car next to him. If he scratches another car, he leaves a note, including his phone number, on the car's windshield.

————

Unless his own safety or the safety of others is at stake, a gentleman resists every urge toward backseat-driving.

All Lit Up

As more and more state and local governments place increasingly strict limitations on cigarette, cigar, and pipe smoking in public places—and as concerns increase about the health hazards of smoking, both to smokers themselves and to the people around them—a gentleman smoker may find himself faced with increasingly complex etiquette challenges in an increasingly nonsmoking world.

Even before "No Smoking" signs became nearly universal, a gentleman always took care not to offend others as he indulged his habit. Although smoking is still allowed in the bars of some restaurants and at many outdoor activities such as ball games and stadium concerts, the long-standing rules of common courtesy still pertain.

A gentleman asks the persons sitting beside him, "Do you mind if I smoke?" (If they say, "No. Go right ahead," he feels free to light up. If one of them says, "Actually, I'd prefer that you didn't," he puts away his cigarettes and his matches or lighter.) In no case does he allow his smoke to drift into others' faces. He does not wave his cigar or cigarette in the air, lest he scatter his companions and their clothes with ashes. If he is a smoker, a gentleman takes every possible precaution to avoid "ashtray breath." He brushes his teeth regularly and makes frequent use of breath mints and mouthwash.

A gentleman never smokes in an elevator. Even if he is going up only one floor. Even if he is alone.

If he finds himself among a clutch of smokers who have retreated to the doorway of a restaurant or any other public building, he still does his best to prevent clouds of smoke from drifting into the faces of passersby.

In every case, and no matter how fiercely he may be longing to light up, he follows the rules of the house. If he sees a sign that says "Smoking Is Not Permitted," he honors it—whether he discovers it in a theater lobby, on the menu at a restaurant, or even on a sign on a sidewalk. If he has not noticed the signage, and if he is asked to put out his cigarette, cigar, or pipe, he does so immediately.

If he is staying in a hotel with a no-smoking policy, he respects that policy. If he is a smoker and discovers that he has been booked in a nonsmoking room, he asks to be moved to another room, if one is available.

If a gentleman is a guest in a private home where no ashtrays have been provided, he does not even broach the subject of smoking, and he certainly does not resort to flicking his ashes into a saucer or the closest available flower pot. In such cases, if a gentleman feels that he really must smoke, he simply says, "If you don't mind, I'm going to step outside. I think I'd like a smoke."

Cigar smoking creates even more specific challenges. A gentleman may be a connoisseur of fine tobaccos. He may savor his cigar in the same way that he savors a glass of good whiskey (which is to say, only on occasion, and never to excess). He recognizes, however, that cigar smoking, for many people, is an acquired taste and that, to some nonsmokers, cigar fumes may be even more repellent than cigarette smoke.

Before smoking, he always checks to make sure cigars are permitted. Once his cigar is lit, he does not puff so that noxious clouds of smoke surround his face, and he does not allow his cigar to accumulate a long, fragile column of ash that may shatter, spoiling his shirtfront or the table linens.

As an alternative to smoking, a gentleman may elect to keep an unlit cigar clenched between his teeth. If he does so, he makes sure to keep the sodden stump of his stogie in his mouth, so that he does not share its unsightliness with others. If he opts for chewing tobacco, he does so outside. He does not keep a drool cup on his desk. He does not spit on the street.

Given the new emphasis on smoke-free environments, however, nonsmokers have their own responsibilities as well. If a gentleman finds tobacco smoke repellent, or if it makes him physically ill, he avoids places where smoking is permitted. If he is asked, "Do you mind if I have a cigarette?" he answers the question forthrightly, and unjudgmentally, saying, "Thank you so much for asking. I'd really prefer that you didn't."

If he discovers that a smoker has lit up in a public place where smoking is not permitted, he does not take the matter into his own hands. Instead, he alerts the building manager, the host of the restaurant, or the nearest security guard.

If a gentleman prefers that people not smoke in his house or apartment, he does not sermonize or moralize about the subject. He simply puts the ashtrays away.

International Relations

In business, on the street, or in social life, a gentleman may often encounter or be introduced to people for whom English is not their native language. He understands that this is simply a fact of modern life.

Because he may have traveled abroad himself, he knows how difficult it may be to be understood in a foreign language. Accordingly, he does not condescend to people who do not speak English. He simply says, "I'm sorry, but I'm not quite sure I'm catching that. Is there somebody here who could help us out?" His new acquaintance may not actually understand what the gentleman is saying, but his good intentions will be evident, even if only by his tone of voice. The two of them may fumble and have fun with their misunderstanding initially, but there will ultimately come a point at which the gentleman will have to say, "It's been awfully nice meeting you," or "Would you like to go to the bar for another drink?" or, most simply, "I'll be moving on now." A nod of the head, as a gesture of greeting or kindly farewell, serves well in almost any language.

On the other hand, if a gentleman is introducing two people who do not speak the same language, he does his best to serve as interpreter. Especially if he has brought the non-English-speaking person to the party, he never leaves his friend alone, unless it appears his friend has struck up some sort of conversation with another guest—at which point the gentleman may take a breather.

On the street corner, at a deli, or at the checkout counter of his local grocery, a gentleman will frequently meet people who speak different languages and who come from different cultures. In such circumstances, a gentleman is patient and treats the non-English speakers with all due respect. He understands that when two people do not speak the same language, there is likely to be frustration on both sides of the non-conversation. Therefore, he does not raise his voice at other people simply because they do not speak his native language.

If a gentleman is in daily contact with people who do not speak English, he may wish to learn a few words of their language, so that he can at least say, "good morning" and "please" and "thank you." He does not attempt to force them to learn English, but if it appears that they would appreciate a bit of assistance in communicating with others, he does his best to help.

A gentleman holds his temper when dealing with service representatives on the phone, no matter what language they speak. He knows that arguing with an anonymous person on the other end of a telephone line will get him nowhere and will very likely imperil the quality of service he receives.

———

When doing business on the phone or in person, if the conflict of languages is causing confusion, a gentleman asks to speak to an English-speaking supervisor.

———

If a gentleman receives an unwanted telephone solicitation, he simply says, "I do not accept this sort of telephone call. Please do not call me again."

———

If the hour is terribly early or extremely late, a gentleman does not phone a private residence.

A gentleman turns down the television, and the sound system, after ten o'clock. If he must listen to music at three o'clock in the morning, he buys himself a good pair of headphones.

Taking Flight

Almost invariably, the passengers in line in the concourse of an airport have been brought together by a mix of chance and necessity. A gentleman understands that in such situations, it is important for everyone to abide by the shared rules.

Upon arriving at the airport, prior to his departure, a gentleman immediately proceeds to the airline counter to check his bags (unless he is traveling with carry-on luggage only). He knows that, if he is traveling abroad, his luggage may be subjected to extra scrutiny. He submits to this process with all good grace. He does not slow down the process or harass the security personnel by shouting, "Hey, watch it! You're wrinkling my T-shirts."

As his line moves closer to the security checkpoint, he proceeds with removing his shoes, his belt, his hat or cap, and his coat, if he is wearing one. He places all these items, as well as his pocket change, his watch, his money clip, his cell phone, and his laptop (if he is carrying one), in the bins provided by the security personnel.

If, for some reason, the security personnel must open the gentleman's carry-on bags for an additional safety check, or if they must subject him to an additional body screening, he does not grouse, "What's this about? Do I look like some kind of *bomber*?" Neither does he attempt to make jokes about terrorism and airplane disasters. Such remarks, if overheard by security personnel, who almost certainly will not find them amusing, may lead to his being removed from his flight.

When it is time for him to board his flight, he quietly takes his place in line and waits for his seat number to be called.

On the Wing

Once a gentleman's flight has left the ground, he remains a customer of the airline and can expect courteous, efficient service from them. But he also has become, for the coming hours, a member of a small community, a community that has its own rules and its own codes of behavior.

It does not matter whether a gentleman is flying first class, business class, or coach. He does his best to comply with the requests and instructions of the flight attendants, to help guarantee a safe, pleasant flight for himself and his fellow passengers. He turns off his electronic equipment even before he is asked to do so, and he remains quiet and attentive while the flight attendants explain the procedures to be followed in case of an emergency. He will be wise to make a last-minute visit to the restroom since, especially on some flights departing from major U.S. cities, passengers may be required to remain in their seats for the first thirty minutes of the flight.

If carry-on bags are permitted on his flight, a gentleman makes sure they fit easily into the overhead bins in the cabin. He does his best not to force the line of passengers behind him to back up while he struggles with an oversized bag. If he realizes that he is indeed blocking the aisle, he simply says, "I'm sorry," to the people behind him. If he realizes that his bag is unlikely to fit in the bin, he sets it temporarily in his seat, steps out of the aisle, and waits until a flight attendant is available to assist him.

If he notices that a fellow passenger is having difficulty stowing his or her bag, and if he is tall enough and agile enough to be of real assistance, he offers a hand to help push the bag into the bin. He does not demean a fellow passenger by muttering, "Hey, why don't you move it, sister," or "What's the matter? Do you think you're the only person on this plane?"

Once his flight has left the airport, a gentleman remains in his seat, with his seatbelt fastened, unless he must make a trip to the restroom. Unless he has a circulatory problem that makes it risky for him to remain seated for extended periods, he does not roam up and down the aisles, chatting with friends and obstructing the path of the flight attendants and the beverage cart.

On a flight of any duration, a gentleman does not attempt to force his fellow passengers to engage in conversation with him. A cordial "Hello, how are you?" is all he really needs to say. If the fellow passenger seems interested in pursuing a conversation, he may proceed to make pleasant small talk. In no case does he allow the conversation to grow so loud as to intrude on the privacy of other passengers.

If he has brought along his MP3 player, or other personal entertainment system, he keeps the volume turned to a reasonable level, knowing that, although he may be wearing his earbuds, the sound can still disturb the peace of his fellow flyers.

Although a gentleman may find it difficult to sleep during any flight, he realizes that others may wish to get as much rest as possible during the course of the trip. He remains quiet and does his best to stay within the confines of his seat. If he wishes to read, he keeps his reading light turned to the lowest level he finds usable. He does not attempt to soothe his restlessness by too-frequent purchases from the beverage cart.

If it turns out that flight regulations prevent him from bringing toothpaste on board, a gentleman may wish to equip himself with a goodly stash of breath mints. If he is an inveterate tooth-brusher, he will bring along a toothbrush (provided it passes the security check) so that he can give his teeth a fresh brush, at least once across the course of an extended flight.

As the flight nears its destination, he once again follows the directions of the flight attendants. He does not leap up from his seat or start yammering into his cell phone the second the plane has landed. Instead, he takes his place in line, along with the other passengers, pulling his carry-on bag from the bin as swiftly and as carefully as possible. He does not want to hold up the line, but neither does he want to risk causing the passenger behind him to suffer a concussion.

In all cases, while he is on a plane, just as when he is in an airport, a gentleman understands that all

A GENTLEMAN EXPERIENCES REAL LIFE

passengers are expected to abide by the safety rules and restrictions. He knows that they are not directed specifically at him. On the other hand, if he notices that another passenger is involved in what may be risky behavior, or if another passenger seems to be in distress, he proceeds to alert a flight attendant, as soon as possible.

At sporting events, a gentleman does not begrudge the other team its victory. If his own team is the victor, he does not taunt the opposition.

————

If a gentleman borrows another person's property—whether it is a power drill, a new best seller, or a set of salad forks—he sets a deadline by which he plans to return it. He keeps to that deadline and returns the property in good condition.

————

If a gentleman is around another person's dog, he does not tease that dog or encourage it to bark.

————

A gentleman does not pick up other people's babies, unless he is invited to do so. Neither does he overexcite children of any age.

A gentleman always carries dollar bills in his pocket. He never knows when he may need to tip a doorman, a maître d', or a parking attendant. He even carries a few extra singles to lend to other gentlemen or ladies who may be caught unprepared.

———

A gentleman never feels that he must say pleasant things about unpleasant people. Even when describing pleasant people, he does not stretch the truth. Goodness, when accurately described, can stand on its own.

———

If a gentleman must leave the dinner table, he simply says, "Excuse me." It does not matter whether he is headed for the bathroom or to make a phone call. No further explanation is necessary.

A Gentleman and His E-mail

For many a gentleman, his e-mail is a part of his daily life—at home, at the office, or even on the sidewalk (provided he can check it by using his cell phone). A gentleman may revel in the swiftness with which it allows him to communicate with others. Nevertheless, he does not use the wonders of modern technology as an excuse to ignore every vestige of good manners.

Whenever a gentleman sends an e-mail, he is careful what he says—perhaps even more careful than he would be when drafting a traditional handwritten or typewriter-typed letter. He understands that, although he may designate an e-mail as "Confidential," he has no guarantee that it will be handled that way. He knows that e-mails may be easily forwarded to dozens, even hundreds, of people. Thus, before he hits the Send button on his laptop, he meticulously reviews his message, editing it if necessary, but always doing his best to make sure the recipient of the message will understand precisely what the gentleman meant to say—and the tone in which he meant to say it.

A gentleman makes it a personal rule never to send an e-mail in a fit of anger. On any occasion when he sits down at his keyboard, he tries his best to be calm, articulate, and sober. He knows that an angry letter may rest overnight before it is posted, giving the gentleman an opportunity to reread it, rethink it, and destroy it, should that seem the right thing to do. Angry e-mails are all too often shared and forwarded. Apologetic e-mails seldom are.

When e-mails are written on the fly—or in the heat of the moment—the recipient may not understand the sender's true intentions, particularly if the subject matter is sensitive in nature. In almost every case, such subject matter is probably better handled by phone or, best of all, in person.

Although an e-mail is a form of written correspondence, it does not nesessarily take the place of a hard-copy letter or a handwritten note. In his social life, a gentleman may find it convenient to use his e-mail in almost any situation in which a telephone call or a voice-mail message would usually suffice. A quick e-mail saying, "Enjoyed drinks last night. Let's try to get together again next week," or "Thanks so much for picking me up yesterday at the repair shop. You were a real lifesaver," can do the job. Meanwhile, although an e-mail saying, "Suzette and I enjoyed the dinner, and you were so nice to treat us to the movie," may be a sincere expression of a gentleman's gratitude, it still cannot approach the thoughtfulness or graciousness of a handwritten note or a voice-to-voice phone call.

On the other hand, a gentleman may find e-mail to be of ready assistance in some of life's most challenging social situations. As soon as he hears about the death of a friend, he is perfectly right to send a simple, direct message immediately, saying, "I've just heard about Edwin. I am so sorry. I'll try to call you tonight." But he must then follow up with the actual phone call, as promised. He never uses an e-mail as a shield against the awkwardness of a potentially difficult moment.

After he has sent an e-mail message to a personal friend, a gentleman does not assume that his friend will respond to him within twenty-four hours.

————

A gentleman remembers that, although the Internet has made the world smaller, people still live in different time zones.

————

A gentleman starts off each of his e-mails—at least those of a personal nature—with a traditional salutation. He writes, "Dear Sally," rather than, "Hi Sally," or simply "Sally," or "Hey!!!"

————

If the sender of an e-mail message asks a gentleman to respond to him by phone, rather than by e-mail, a gentleman complies with that request.

A gentleman ends each of his e-mail messages with an appropriate closing. He may say, at the end, "All thanks," "Thank you," "Sincerely," or in the most intimate communications, he may add "xoxo," the age-old sign for "hugs and kisses." At any rate, he always adds a closure that indicates his message is done. A gentleman always adds his name at the end of his messages.

———————

A gentleman is wary of hitting the Reply All button when replying to any message that will be shared with a number of people. He does not clutter up the Inbox of dozens of others with a flippant little "OK" or "Works for me!" message that actually pertains to only one person.

———————

If a gentleman is on a tight schedule, he does not attempt to set up appointments via e-mail. Instead, he makes a traditional phone call. His concern, after all, is not whether the message has been *received*. What he needs to know is whether the message has been *heard*.

A gentleman knows how to make a grilled cheese sandwich at two o'clock in the morning and how to make an omelet at seven.

————

A gentleman does not adjust his crotch in public.

————

A gentleman never makes a date out of desperation.

A Gentleman Walks
through a Door

A gentleman always glances behind him when he walks through a door. He never slams a door in another person's face. It does not matter whether the other person is a man or a woman.

If it is a revolving door, a gentleman pays more attention than usual. He steps ahead, does not move too fast, pushes the door open, and makes the world a little easier for the person after him. He never shares a revolving door section with other people. He respects their space. Besides, in big cities, it is in such close quarters that pickpockets do their business.

If a gentleman is approaching a door ahead of another person who is burdened down with packages, or if the door is a heavy one, he offers his assistance, without comment, and without waiting for a "thank you."

A gentleman is considerate of the special needs of senior citizens and people with physical challenges. For example, if he encounters a blind person who seems confused by a busy street corner, he asks, "May I help you across to the sidewalk?" If the offer is accepted, the gentleman provides a helpful hand. If the offer is declined, he maintains his distance, keeping a watchful eye.

———

Whether he is walking on a sidewalk, walking down a hallway, or walking down or up a flight of stairs, a gentleman always keeps to the right.

———

On a rainy day, a gentleman will extend a hand to help anyone over a mud puddle.

———

A gentleman always has an umbrella to share.

Chapter Two

A GENTLEMAN GETS DRESSED

No matter what his age, a gentleman does not let his pants slip below his waist. Unless he is being photographed for an advertisement, he does not expose his underwear in public.

———

In warm weather a gentleman always wears an undershirt.

———

Unless he is a Texas Ranger or a cattle rancher, a gentleman does not wear cowboy boots with a suit.

A gentleman's pants cuffs fall in a gentle break over his shoes. When he stands, his socks do not show.

————————

When a gentleman wears a double-breasted suit or a double-breasted sports coat, he never leaves his jacket unbuttoned.

————————

A gentleman clips his nose hairs and the unsightly hair in his ears. As he grows older, he may also find it necessary to trim his eyebrows.

————————

As he grows older, a gentleman invests in a battery-operated hair trimmer so that he does not have to subject himself to the pain of plucking his nose hairs, much less his ear hairs, by means of a pair of tweezers.

————————

A gentleman does not carry unnecessary paraphernalia in his pockets. A bulky key ring or a Swiss army knife destroys the line of even the most expensive pair of slacks.

When to Wear Brown Shoes

A gentleman knows that even today, black shoes are considered more formal, businesslike, and serious than brown shoes. In fact, in certain businesses—the legal profession, for instance, or the upper echelons of banking—black shoes remain the only truly acceptable footwear.

On the other hand, if a gentleman is in a situation where a brown or green suit or a sports coat would be acceptable—in an office with a more relaxed dress code or at a dressy sporting event, for example—his brown shoes will serve him well. In the heat of summer, he may even resort to a pair of white bucks or—if he wishes to come off as particularly dapper—a pair of the two-toned Oxfords known as "spectators." But only a gentleman with the greatest self-assurance attempts such a feat, and then only at the most sporty of occasions. If a gentleman has any doubts at all about his choice of shoes, he does not allow himself to be swayed by an overly insistent salesperson. He heeds his own instincts. If dark shoes are the shoes in which he feels comfortable, dark shoes are the only shoes he wears.

No matter what the fashion trends of the moment may be, a gentleman never wears brown shoes to a funeral or to a wedding. If he is fortunate enough to have a long life, he will live through many weekends, and his brown loafers will get plenty of wear on any number of other occasions.

How to Shine a Pair of Shoes

1. Sprinkle a few drops of warm water over the polish. Spit works just fine.
2. Cover a finger, or a couple of fingers, with a soft cloth (an old T-shirt is perfect), and use it to work the water into the polish.
3. Apply the polish to the shoe.
4. Work the polish into the leather.
5. Using a clean section of the cloth, or a soft brush, buff the leather to a brilliant shine.

Although a gentleman knows how to polish his own shoes, when he is on a business trip, or when he realizes that his shoes have become scuffed in the midst of a business day, a gentleman patronizes a reputable shoe-shine stand.

A Gentleman and His Cologne

A gentleman considers cologne to be intimate apparel. He knows that it should not cause comment, positive or negative, among other people in the room. Instead, it should be saved as a pleasant surprise for people with whom he makes close physical contact. A gentleman does not use his cologne as a substitute for deodorant. A dab on either side of the neck is quite enough.

When used to excess, cologne is annoying and raises questions about what smells are being covered up. Any time a person can identify the brand of scent that a man is wearing, he is wearing too much. In fact, if a gentleman realizes that he himself can still smell his own cologne, fifteen minutes after he has put it on, he makes a quick trip to the men's room and gives himself a quick scrub with soap and a damp washcloth.

If there is no polish involved, a gentleman occasionally has a manicure.

———————

When the weather is cold, a gentleman always wears gloves, and not just to keep his hands warm. He knows that cold fingers do not make for a pleasant handshake.

———————

Although a gentleman knows where to find a dependable, high-quality dry cleaner, he takes his clothes to the dry cleaner as seldom as possible, knowing that chemicals, no matter how gently used, will shorten the life span of his wardrobe.

———————

A gentleman always lets his suit jacket or sports coat air out overnight before he returns it to the closet.

A gentleman puts his winter clothes, especially his woolens, into storage for the summer months.

———

A gentleman's socks always match, or at least complement, his trousers–not his shirt, his tie, or his pocket-handkerchief.

———

A gentleman feels no necessity to wear socks after Memorial Day–at least in casual situations. If he is Southern, he may not even wear them to church.

———

Despite the impact of global warming, a gentleman still resists any temptation to wear linen before Memorial Day.

A Gentleman and His Cap

A gentleman may well own a stack of baseball caps, which he wears after work or even on weekend days at the office. He may feel that a beloved baseball cap is almost a part of his body, but he never forgets that it is still a hat and that common courtesy demands it be treated as such.

A gentleman does not wear his cap inside most public buildings—especially houses of worship. He need not remove his cap, or any other hat, in the lobby of an office building, in a department store, or in the grocery. Neither does he feel the need to remove it in an elevator. However, he does remove any sort of headgear once he has entered the waiting room of a doctor's office or a lawyer's office, or whenever he is making personal contact with another person, such as a teller at the bank or a clerk at a department store.

Traditionally, a gentleman would remove his hat if he were greeting a woman or being introduced to a new acquaintance of either sex. However, if the weather is foul, or if a man wears a cap to cover up an unwashed mass of hair or to disguise a balding head, he need not remove it. He tips his cap, giving its brim a quick tug, out of respect for the other person—and as a wistful acknowledgment of courtesy long past.

In no case does a gentleman wear a cap or hat when he is at any meal that is served indoors, even if it is being served at a bar. Simply turning the bill of his cap backwards does not take care of the situation. He removes his cap so that others can see his face and be assured that they are enjoying his full attention.

If a gentleman is given to wearing outlandish hats—such as a deerstalker or a Russian sable cap with earflaps—he understands that he will probably attract the attention, and lead to the amusement, of others.

———

A gentleman washes his hair regularly; he makes every effort to prevent dandruff.

———

If a gentleman feels the urge to color his mustache, he shaves his mustache off.

———

A gentleman never wears a belt when he is wearing suspenders.

———

When a gentleman wears his black tie with a wing-collar shirt, he always positions the points of the collar *behind* the tie. That way, the ends of the tie can help hold the stiffened collar down.

Once he is past the age of ten, a gentleman ties his own tie. Especially if it is a bow tie. Especially if it is black.

A gentleman never wears a button-down collar with a bow tie.

Even if a gentleman has to rent his dinner clothes, he wears something that is not borrowed. A good pair of cufflinks is enough.

A gentleman's shirt studs need not match his cufflinks precisely. However, they always complement each other.

When a gentleman wears a cummerbund, he makes sure the pleats are turned upward. (In that way, they can actually be used as tiny, secret pockets, perhaps for the safekeeping of theatre tickets, a stub from the coatroom, or a tip for the washroom attendant.)

When to Wear a Tuxedo

A gentleman never wears a tuxedo before five o'clock, no matter what anyone else does. If he owns his dinner clothes—the correct term for what is known as a tuxedo—he wears them anytime the invitation says "black tie" or "black tie optional." Likewise, if he is attending any formal event—a wedding reception or a dance—that begins after seven in the evening, he may assume that black tie is appropriate.

However, if he knows that other guests at the party are unlikely to be dressed in dinner clothes, he plays it safe and wears a dark suit. If the invitation does not indicate any dress code, or if "black tie optional" is suggested, a gentleman does not feel obligated to rent dinner clothes. In such situations, his dark suit will serve him perfectly well.

If he does choose to rent his dinner clothes, a gentleman makes sure to visit the rental store in order to make his selection and place his order well ahead of time. (During busy times of the year, such as the holidays or in the springtime wedding season, he may find the selections limited, both style-wise and size-wise.) He picks up his suit at least forty-eight hours before he will need it, on the off-chance that the necessary alterations may not have been made.

If a gentleman finds that he is renting formalwear with any regularity, he will be wise—in terms of both economy and convenience—to purchase his own suit.

A gentleman is wary of ordering "heavy starch" at the laundry, since it almost invariably leads to the swifter deterioration of this fabric.

Renting Formalwear

If a gentleman is only rarely invited to black-tie affairs, he may find it more convenient to rent his formalwear. When he rents black tie, however, he undertakes the mission as seriously as if he were purchasing the suit for long-term wear. On such occasions, he is wise to observe the following precautions:

1. *Plan ahead*. A gentleman does not wait until the last moment to handle such a serious matter. He consults friends as to the reputations of various rental establishments, perhaps even visiting the stores to ask about their rental fees, rental-return policies, and the time required for the suit to be tailored after the fitting. (A gentleman never assumes that he might simply stroll in and out of the store with a suit casually picked from the rack.)
2. *Choose black*. Nothing else works. Nothing else is right. Nothing else need be said.
3. *Pick it up early*. A wise gentleman picks up his rental finery at least two days before the event, giving himself

plenty of time to try on the jacket and trousers to make sure they have been altered according to plan.

4. *Try it on, then and there*. An even wiser gentleman tries on his suit before ever leaving the store. He also checks to be sure all accessories, including cufflinks and studs, shoes, and cummerbund, are in order.

5. *Turn it in on time*. A wise gentleman makes sure he is aware of the return deadline, to avoid extra costs and unpleasant surprises.

6. *Consider buying it*. Most quality rental establishments also sell formalwear. Many such establishments mount annual sales at which lightly used suits may be purchased at greatly reduced prices.

How to Tie a Bow Tie

Tying a bow tie is, essentially, like tying any other bow. A gentleman knows this, and he does not become frustrated if he fumbles the first few times he attempts the procedure. Instead, he gives himself enough practice at home when he does not have a pressing dinner date.

1. Adjust the length of the tie. (A shorter tie will result in a smaller bow. If the tie is left long, the end product has a fluffier, less-tailored look. Either look is perfectly acceptable, provided it is flattering to the gentleman wearing it.)

2. Put the tie around your neck. Leave one end hanging longer than the other.

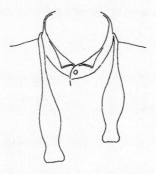

3. Bring the long end of the tie over the short end. Then pull it up from behind, just as if you were beginning a granny knot.

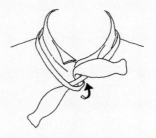

4. Tug securely on both ends.

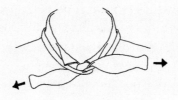

5. Fold the short end of the tie over to make a loop.

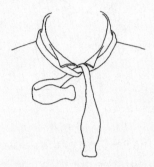

6. Bring the long end of the tie up, over, and around the middle of the entire package.

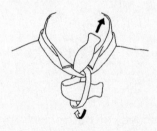

7. Fold the remaining part of the long end into a loop and stuff it through the opening behind the short end. (The loop of the long end must end up behind the flat part of the short end.)

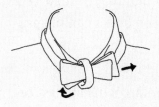

8. Tug on the tie and twist it about until
   it takes on a neatly finished look.
   (This step may take some time, but
   do not give up. It really will work. Take
   care, however, to tug on both loops
   at the same time, just as if you were
   tightening your shoelaces. Otherwise,
   the bow will come undone.)

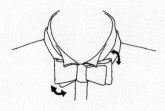

Although a gentleman usually takes his shirts to a laundry, he also knows how to use an iron and a can of spray starch.

————

A gentleman owns at least one pair of black lace-up shoes.

————

When a gentleman wears a vest, he leaves the bottom button undone.

————

When a gentleman outgrows his clothes, he gives them away to charity. He does not pretend that someday he will lose weight. When, and if, he does lose weight, he certainly will not want to celebrate by wearing out-of-date coats and trousers.

————

When necessary, a gentleman has his shoes resoled and the heels replaced. He recognizes that this is not simply a matter of appearance; it is also the best way to preserve his high-priced footwear.

A gentleman never wears the same pair
of blue jeans two days in a row. He knows
that common hygiene and common
courtesy demand that they rest for a good
twenty-four hours between wearings.

———

A gentleman's pants are always cuffed,
except for his casual khakis, his blue
jeans, and his formal trousers.

———

A gentleman never has creases ironed
into the legs of his jeans.

———

Whenever a gentleman goes to the theater,
to a religious service, or to a restaurant,
he tucks his shirttail in. Although an
untucked shirttail may be the style of
the moment, a gentleman knows that his
tucked-in shirttail is timeless.

A gentleman knows that a pierced nose or a pierced ear can heal with the passing of the years, while a tattoo will be with him for a lifetime.

Chapter Three

A GENTLEMAN GOES TO DINNER

If a gentleman wishes to eat the garnish
on his dinner plate, he does so.

———

After business hours, a gentleman turns
his cell phone to the vibrate mode as soon
as he is seated at his table at a restaurant.
He does not check his text messages,
much less send text messages, while
seated at the table.

———

A gentleman follows the same protocol
when dining in a private home—even if
it is his own home, and especially if he
is serving as host.

The Tipping Point

Tipping is a delicate matter that concerns only the gentleman and the server. He does not brag about leaving a generous gratuity. If the service has been inferior, a gentleman does not inform his companions that he plans to leave a less-than-sizable tip.

A gentleman leaves a tip in a restaurant or a bar—including coffee bars—but he is under no constraint to do so at a fast-food establishment. To recognize good service, he leaves at least 15 percent of his total bill. Excellent, attentive service justifies a tip of 20 percent or more. If the service has been minimally acceptable, however, a gentleman may leave only 10 percent. If he is so dissatisfied that he feels the urge to leave less, he leaves nothing and explains his actions to the manager. Angrily leaving a dime or a quarter demonstrates that the customer and the server are equally ill mannered.

When determining his tip, a gentleman must decide for himself whether he wishes to tip on the final total of his bill or on the pretax total, which includes only the cost of his food and drink. Although he may sometimes find it difficult to separate the tax from his total bill, a gentleman feels no necessity to tip on the percentage of his tab that is headed for the government coffers. He may simply find it more convenient to tip on the total bill, but that decision is his, and his alone. He need not explain it to his server or to his fellow diners.

In an upscale restaurant ("upscale" being defined by entrées costing in excess of thirty dollars and by fine linen cloths on the tables), a gentleman can often be expected to provide a gratuity for the wine steward, who will assist in the selection of wines and will present them to the gentleman at his table. The final bill for the meal may include a line for the wine steward's gratuity, or the gentleman may simply tip the wine steward himself, with cash, on his way out of the restaurant. A tip equaling 20 percent of the cost of the wine can get pricey, but it is what is usually expected.

In upscale restaurants, the host, hostess, or maître d' may play an active role in seating the gentleman's party, explaining the menu, and ensuring that their dining experience goes as smoothly as possible. In such cases, a gentleman quietly slips the host, hostess, or maître d' twenty dollars or more as his party prepares to leave the restaurant.

In midscale restaurants, where the host or hostess is simply responsible for leading a gentleman and his party to their table, no tip is expected.

On occasion, a gentleman may encounter a tip jar next to the cash register in a coffee bar or some other restaurant that does not offer table service. A gentleman understands that the tips he leaves in this jar are to be shared by the restaurant's behind-the-scenes staff as well as the frontline staff at the register. He may wish to leave 10 or 15 percent of his total bill; he may choose to leave a dollar. He may decide to drop his pocket change in the jar or elect to leave nothing. The choice is entirely his own, but if he dines at an establishment with any frequency, he will manage to leave a little something in the tip jar, at least from time to time.

When visiting a bar at an event held in a public place, such as a hotel ballroom or a convention center, a gentleman may discover that the bartender has placed a glass, with a few dollar bills stuffed in it, discreetly behind the bar—but not so discreetly that patrons will miss seeing it. When a gentleman sees a tip glass, he infers that tips are permitted and even encouraged. (At some events, servers are not allowed to solicit tips since their gratuities will be included in the final bill presented to the event's organizers.) If he chooses to tip his bartender, he simply places a dollar or two in the glass or he may hand his tip directly to the server.

If he visits the bar with any frequency, and whether he is ordering a cocktail or a soft drink, he tips his bartender at least once. On such occasions, he is tipping simply as a token of appreciation for the service he has received. His tip is not determined by the estimated cost of his drink.

A gentleman never tips the bartenders, or any other servers, at a private party, unless they have offered him some extraordinary assistance—such as helping him tidy up a soiled shirtfront or providing him with a safety pin to mend a ripped trouser leg. In all cases, such tips are provided in the most discreet manner possible. Usually, they are simply "palmed off" to the helpful server as part of a thank-you handshake.

As in the rest of life, a gentleman's goal in tipping is to be appreciative and appropriate. When settling on the size of his tip, a gentleman hopes not to appear chintzy. Neither is he overly extravagant.

KNOWING WHAT TO LEAVE:

A Trustworthy Guide to the Tip

Server in a midscale to upscale restaurant	15 to 20 percent for attentive service
Server in a casual restaurant, such as a diner or soda shop	15 to 20 percent for attentive service
Barista in a coffee bar	$1
Wine steward in an upscale restaurant	20 percent of the cost of the wine
Host in an upscale restaurant	$20 or more, depending on the extent, and attentiveness, of the service
Men's room attendant	$3 or more, each visit
Valet parker	$3 to $5
Doorman	$5 for assistance in hailing a cab
Cash register tip jar	$1 or $2
Bartender at a large social event	$1 or $2 per drink, if tip glass is provided
Bartender or server in a private home	Nothing, unless special assistance has been provided

If the food set before him is intended to be eaten piping hot (or icy cold), and if a gentleman is the first person to be served at his table, he waits for one other person to be served before he begins to eat.

———

If a gentleman and his fellow diners are all served at the same time, and if there is a lady at the table, he waits until she lifts her fork before he takes his first bite.

———

If a gentleman's meal is slow to arrive from the kitchen, and if others at the table have been served, he urges them, "Please, go ahead without me." And he means it.

———

A gentleman does not stack his plates at the end of the meal.

———

A gentleman does not cut up all his food at once.

When a gentleman has finished eating, he places his knife and his fork on his plate side by side, as if they were the hands of a clock set at 5:25. He never places a piece of dirty flatware back on the table.

―――――――

A gentleman never salts his food before tasting it. He would never insult the cook in that way.

―――――――

When a gentleman has an unpleasant time in a restaurant, he does not badger the waitstaff. He lodges his complaint with the management. Unless he is a glutton for punishment, he does not patronize that restaurant again.

How to Know Which Fork to Use

If the table has been set correctly, a gentleman has no problem knowing which fork, spoon, or knife to pick up first. When he sits down at the table, he will find his flatware and his cutlery set out in the order in which he will need them. When the first course arrives, he uses the fork that is the farthest away from his plate. When he is finished with that course, he leaves his fork on his plate, and it is taken away. He proceeds in the same manner throughout the meal so that by the time dessert rolls around, he will have only one fork, spoon, or knife left. If by chance the flatware has been arranged in the wrong order, a gentleman still follows this logical system. In such cases, the person setting the table has caused the confusion.

Limited Offerings

Even if a gentleman is an inveterate steak eater, he is likely to find himself playing host to people who choose not to eat meat. (Sometimes, they will scorn all meat, even all dairy products. Or they may limit themselves to white meats, such as fish and chicken.) When a gentleman entertains guests who are vegetarians, he attempts to honor their wishes and make sure they enjoy an appetizing, satisfying meal. When selecting a restaurant, he checks to make sure the menu includes a variety of salads and pasta dishes. If he is selecting a menu ahead of time, he arranges to have a vegetarian option available.

If a gentleman himself is a vegetarian, he does not ask to be coddled. He informs his host or hostess ahead of time, so that the proper arrangements can be made. When he accepts an invitation, he may say, "Of course, I'd love to come for dinner on Saturday. I'm a vegetarian, you know, but otherwise, I'll eat anything that's set before me." For better or worse, the vegetarian usually is the exception to the rule. It is his responsibility to let his host or hostess know about his special needs.

In all cases, a gentleman respects the dietary restrictions of others, whether they are imposed for reasons of health, religion, or political conviction. He does not attempt to force them to go against their convictions or to risk spending a night in the emergency room. A gentleman would never say, "Come on. Try the shrimp. It's not gonna kill you."

A gentleman does not lean
back in his chair.

————

If a gentleman is on a diet, he does not
talk about it at the table.

How to Make a Dinner Reservation

A gentleman does not make dinner reservations unless he actually plans to use them. If he must cancel or if the size of his party changes, he informs the restaurant as far ahead of time as possible. A gentleman knows that people who do not claim their reservations will quickly gain an unsavory reputation.

A gentleman does not take it as a personal affront if a restaurant is unable to seat his party at the time he requests. If he is unable to accept the hour that is offered, he asks for a recommendation of another establishment.

If his party has special requirements—seating in a nonsmoking area or wheelchair access, for example—he makes those requests when he reserves the table.

If he is not sure whether a jacket is required, he inquires about the restaurant's dress code ahead of time.

Tradition holds that it is permissible for a gentleman and his party to arrive up to fifteen minutes late to claim their reservation. If they arrive any later without having informed the restaurant, however, they may very well learn that their table has been given up to another party.

On the other hand, if a gentleman and his party arrive on time and are asked to wait more than fifteen minutes—and if they are not content to bide their time in the bar—a gentleman has every right to ask the restaurant's host to assist him in securing a table at another restaurant, of the same quality, in the same vicinity.

A gentleman understands the vicissitudes of restaurant management, and he understands that parties of well-served, contented diners may wish to linger at their tables, chatting over their coffee or cognac. But a gentleman also knows that an overlong wait can do irreparable damage to what might have been a delightful evening.

How to Order a
Bottle of Wine

A gentleman orders a wine he likes or a wine suggested by a server or by one of his dinner companions. That does not mean that he must order the most expensive wine on the list. When a suggested wine is out of his price range, he orders something else, with no apologies to anyone. He may simply say, "That sounds lovely, but it may be a little out of my price range," or he may say, "I was thinking of something more in the range of the Pretty Hills Chardonnay. What would you suggest in that range?"

In general, red wine is still the wine of choice to accompany red meat, pasta dishes with tomato sauces, and most heavy entrées. White wines are usually selected to accompany fish, chicken, salads, and pasta dishes with light sauces. But a gentleman may feel at ease ordering any wine he likes.

When a gentleman has ordered a bottle of wine, it will be presented to him by the server, who will show him the label (so that a gentleman can see that he is, in truth, being served what he ordered) and then offer him the cork (so that a gentleman can see that it is not too dry). The server will then pour a sip of wine in the gentleman's glass. The gentleman performs a quick taste test, and if the wine passes muster, he allows the server to pour it, first for the gentleman's guests and then for the gentleman himself.

The server may leave the wine, if it is white, in a cooler at tableside. If it is red, he may leave it on the table. In either case, a gentleman may wait for the server to return to refill empty glasses or he may take care of that duty himself.

A gentleman does not talk with
his mouth full.

————

When a gentleman pours a glass of
wine, he finishes by turning the bottle
slightly, in order to prevent unsightly
dribbles and drips.

————

A gentleman never crunches on his ice
cubes except in the privacy of his home.

————

A gentleman does not attempt to
change the opinions of his dinner
companions. A seated dinner is not a
debate tournament.

————

A gentleman never drinks a
cocktail through a straw.

How to Use a Dinner Napkin

After a gentleman takes his seat at a dinner table, his first action is always to place his dinner napkin in his lap. He does not tuck it into his belt or under his chin. Neither does he wait for a server to handle his napkin for him. (Only in the most ostentatious restaurants do servers treat the unfurling of napkins as part of a predinner sideshow.)

If a gentleman briefly leaves the table during dinner, he leaves his napkin, loosely folded, in his chair. (Sad to say, in even some fine restaurants, he may return to the table only to discover that a server has refolded the gentleman's soiled napkin and returned it to the table. The restaurant is wrong in this case, not the gentleman.) When a gentleman has finished his meal, he loosely folds his napkin and places it to the side of his plate.

At the dinner table, a gentleman helps the woman to the right of him as she sits or rises from her chair.

————

At a cocktail party or at a seated dinner, if a gentleman discovers that he has put something unpleasant or unpalatable in his mouth, he gets rid of it in the most efficient way possible, using his fingers or his fork, as necessary. He works quickly and does not even attempt to disguise his actions behind a napkin.

————

If a gentleman must park his own car at a restaurant, or any other place of entertainment, he offers to let his passengers out at the door.

————

A gentleman never smokes while he is eating. Ever.

Chapter Four

A GENTLEMAN SAYS THE RIGHT THING

There are certain questions that a gentleman never asks:

- "How do the two of you know each other?"
- "Why do I recognize your name?"
- "You don't remember me, do you?"
- "Would you mind if I look at the label?"
- "Are you going to eat all of that?"

———

A gentleman does not brag.

———

A gentleman does not whine.

A gentleman does not beat
around the bush.

———

A gentleman never knowingly insults
another person; neither does he revel in
the embarrassment of others.

———

A gentleman knows how to
use a dictionary.

———

A gentleman accepts a compliment by
saying, "Thank you. It's nice of you to tell
me that." When a friend tells him, "That's
a good-looking tie, Jim," a gentleman does
not respond by saying, "This old thing? I
was almost ashamed to bring it out." Such
remarks imply that the person paying the
compliment has questionable taste.

THE ART OF THE CONVERSATION

A gentleman need not attempt to engage every person he meets in extended conversation. He attempts to be cordial, or at least congenial, to everyone he encounters—whether it is a new acquaintance at a dinner party or a person who simply asks him for directions on the sidewalk.

Although he may not be the world's most outgoing fellow, he can at least engage in civil discourse with almost anyone, provided he practices a few classic guidelines.

How to Start a Conversation

At a party, a reception, or a business meeting, a gentleman strikes up a conversation with any pleasant person he encounters. To prevent awkwardness, however, he begins with positive, noncontroversial subject matter. In every case, a gentleman begins by asking a question that does not bring the conversation around to himself.

If the person standing next to him

responds cordially, he continues with a few more questions until the conversation is underway. (A gentleman knows, at this point, that he is still testing the waters.) If he finds that the conversation is getting nowhere, after two or three well-meaning questions, spaced out over the course of several minutes, he gives up the quest, at least for the moment, lest it appear that he is attempting to pry.

Never, or at least not until the conversation is well underway, does he venture into uncertain territory, such as the lukewarm food on the buffet or the recent downslide of the company stock. Invariably, after he has made this sort of comment, a gentleman discovers that he is speaking to the hostess's sister or to the boss's son.

Lost for Words

When walking into a crowded reception or arriving at a seated dinner where he is a virtual newcomer, even the most outgoing gentleman may feel like an outsider. For the less than loquacious gentleman, such moments can bring on attacks of panic, speechlessness, and clammy palms. Over the course of time, however, even the most understated, soft-spoken gentleman will learn to make his way through such uncharted waters.

At a large gathering, he does his best not to leave himself standing alone on the edge of the crowd. If there is a bar or a buffet table, he moves toward it, giving himself the best chance possible to make human contact. He may break the ice simply by saying, "May I step in beside you, here in line?" or "Have you already put in your order?" He need not be quick-witted and quotable at such a moment. Unless his new acquaintance greets him with a blank stare or turns a cold shoulder to him, a gentleman may venture forward a bit more boldly.

A short list of all-purpose opening lines includes:

- "This is a nice party, isn't it?"
- "Charlie has certainly done a good job of bringing this meeting together, hasn't he?"
- "These really are beautiful flowers, aren't they?"

- "We're certainly having a full schedule. Have you been able to get to many of the meetings?"

  Or, best of all . . .

- "I'm Gus Tibbetts. I'm from Duluth." Or "I'm Mike Jenner. I'm a friend of Tabitha."

If a gentleman makes this sort of good-faith effort, however, only to find that his new acquaintance—or, even worse, his partner at the dinner table—clearly has no wish to strike up any sort of civil chitchat, he does his best either to move on or to grin and bear his way through the remainder of the evening.

How to Make an Introduction

Even in an increasingly casual society, a gentleman respects the time-honored traditions surrounding social introductions:

- A younger person is always introduced to an older person. For example, when Larry Lyons, who is in his twenties, is introduced to Mr. Allgood, who is in his fifties, a gentleman says, "Mr. Allgood, I'd like you to meet Larry Lyons." Even if a younger woman is being introduced to any older man, a gentleman makes sure to say the older person's name first.
- When a gentleman introduces a man and a woman who appear to be of essentially the same age, he introduces the man to the woman. Thus, if his friends Sally Baldwin and Larry Lyons do not know each other, a gentleman introduces them by saying, "Sally, this is my friend Larry Lyons." Then a gentleman turns to Larry and says, "Larry, this is Sally Baldwin."
- In any situation when a gentleman must introduce two people, and one

of them holds a position of some distinction—either as a public official, a member of the clergy, a senior executive in the gentleman's business, or a guest of honor at the event where all of them are gathered—that person is treated with all due deference. Thus, a gentleman says, "Mr. President (or Madame President), I'd like you to meet Sally Baldwin." Or "Rabbi Rothman, please meet my friend Larry Lyons."

- In all cases, a gentleman feels free to add some detail to stimulate conversation. He might say, for example, "Mr. Allgood, Larry is one of my good friends from law school." Or, "Sally, you may have heard me talk about Larry. We went to the concert at the stadium last week."

- A gentleman makes every effort to pronounce names clearly. If it is convenient, he repeats the names at some not-too-distant point in the conversation.

- If a gentleman finds that he must introduce himself to a person standing next to him at a party, or seated next to him at dinner, he does so by simply saying, "I'm Josh Lowe. How are you this evening?" If he is introducing himself to a fellow gentleman, he offers a ready handshake. If he is introducing himself to a lady, he waits for her to extend her hand.

Even if he is uncertain as to the protocol of the moment, a gentleman does his best to make an introduction. Even if he makes a small mistake, he has not committed the more serious mistake of being rude.

When to Use First Names

Although the world at large is on a first-name basis today, a gentleman knows it is always safe, on first meeting, to address a new acquaintance as "Mr." or "Ms."—especially if he is making his first encounter with that person via telephone or e-mail. He pays particular heed to this guideline if the new acquaintance is an older person or if he is dealing with his superior in a business environment. However, once "Ms. Jones" has told him, "Please, call me Mary," a gentleman concedes to her wish. Otherwise, he runs the risk of making her feel ill at ease.

In general, if a gentleman finds that a person of his own generation is referring to him as "Mr. Brown," he may logically assume that that person wishes to be referred to as "Mr." or "Ms." too. He does not attempt to force business acquaintances to act as if they were his personal friends.

How to End a Conversation

A gentleman recognizes that every conversation has its own natural rhythm. He is not being rude or inconsiderate when he attempts to bring any conversation—no matter how pleasant or how important—to a timely close.

When talking on the telephone, a gentleman accepts the responsibility for ending any conversation he has begun. When the conversation is taking place in his office, it is a gentleman's responsibility to bring the meeting to a close. In every case, he states, as directly as possible, that it is time for the discussion to end; he does not allow the conversation to dawdle along uncomfortably. On the telephone, he may say something as simple as, "It's been very good talking with you, Jack. I hope we get to talk again soon." In person, he stands up, thanks his guest for meeting with him, and extends his hand for a handshake.

Even in a social situation, such as a cocktail party, a gentleman may end a conversation gracefully by saying, "It's been very pleasant talking with you, Mr. Grabbit. I'd like to freshen my drink. Would you care to walk over to the bar along with me?" In doing so, he provides himself with the opportunity to introduce Mr. Grabbit to other people. If Mr. Grabbit declines to accompany him to the bar, a gentleman says, "It really has been nice chatting with you. I hope we get to talk again soon."

A gentleman may employ similar tactics when attempting to bring an end to a pointlessly extended exchange via e-mail or text messaging. He simply says, "Thank you for your help," "Good to hear from you," or "Let's chat again sometime," and then lets that stand as his final contribution to the exchange.

A gentleman gives direct answers, especially to controversial questions. Being direct, however, is not the same thing as being blunt.

————

If a gentleman does not speak French, he does not attempt to use French words.

————

When a gentleman quotes Shakespeare, or any other major author, he does his best to get the quotation right. Otherwise, he leaves Shakespeare out of his conversation.

How to Respond to an Insult

When a gentleman has been subjected to a conscious insult, either in public or in private, his response is simple: because he is a gentleman, he says nothing at all.

————

A gentleman knows it is always best to keep an apology simple.

————

If an apology is sincerely offered, a gentleman accepts it with good grace. He does not pretend that the offense never existed, but he considers it history and moves on. He does not harbor grudges.

How to Say "I'm Sorry"

Although he attempts at all times to be considerate of others, a gentleman sometimes makes mistakes. In such instances, he owns up to his failings and attempts to rectify the wrongdoing before matters grow any worse.

In making his apology, a gentleman is direct and to the point. If he has unintentionally made a remark that has hurt another person's feelings, he may say, "Sam, I'm afraid I said something rude to you last evening at the ball game when we were joking about the color of your shirt. I didn't mean to give offense." If his actions have made another person uncomfortable, he may say, for example, "The other night at the Wallaces', Sally, when I knocked your wineglass out of your hand, I felt like a klutz. I am sorry."

In making an apology, a gentleman does not downplay his error. Neither does he dramatize it.

A gentleman apologizes when he is convinced that he has affronted another person. He does not offer an insincere apology if he has done nothing wrong. That sort of apology is a lie. It is an insult in and of itself.

When a gentleman inconveniences another person by asking him or her to shift so that he can move through a crowded room, he says, "Excuse me." He does not say, "I'm sorry," since there is no reason for him to apologize. In fact, a gentleman never says, "I'm sorry" unless he has given offense.

Wordly Wise

Because he knows that his words often do speak every bit as loudly as his actions, a gentleman monitors his own language and grammar scrupulously, making a conscious effort to avoid certain particularly heinous gaffes.

- A gentleman does not confuse the nominative case with the objective case. For example, he does not say, "Cathy and me want to say thank you for taking us to the movie." But neither does he say, "Thank you for taking Cathy and I to the show."
- A gentleman does not say "ain't." But he also knows it is every bit as ghastly to replace it with "aren't I?" It is no better to say, "I'm getting here late, aren't I?" than it is to say, "I'm the last one here, ain't I?" Instead, he says, "It looks like I'm the first one here for the meeting, am I not?"
- A gentleman does his best not to confuse words that sound alike. For example he does not confuse "picture" with "pitcher." He does not say, "That's a beautiful pitcher on the wall," unless he is actually admiring a vessel intended to hold water.
- A gentleman listens to himself to make sure his pronunciation is as correct as possible. For example, he does not say "axe" (as in "There's something I want to axe you"), when the word he really means to use is "ask."

- A gentleman does not end a sentence with the preposition "at," as in "Where did you get that at?" Instead, he simply asks, "Where did you get that?"
- A gentleman knows the difference between "who" and "whom." ("Who" can serve as the subject of a sentence, a phrase, or a clause. "Whom" is always the object of a verb or a preposition.) In many cases, a gentleman will be tempted to use "whom," in hopes of sounding more proper. He would be wrong to say, "Jerry is the one who we invited." But he would also be wrong—and sound more than a little fussy—to say, "Jerry is the one whom is going with us."
- A gentleman also avoids the fussiness of substituting "myself" for "me." He does not say, "If you have any questions, please contact Dale or myself." Instead, he says, "If you need more information, please get in touch with Dale or me."
- A gentleman does not interrupt the flow of his speech with useless interjections such as "you know," "er," "it's like," or "you know what I mean."

No matter what a gentleman's age or background is, he can always polish his grammar and his pronunciation. He listens closely to himself, avoiding whenever possible the passing slang of the moment. If he plans to say anything worth remembering, he knows it is important to say it right.

How to Write a Sympathy Note

It is appropriate for a gentleman to express sympathy upon the death of someone he has known, admired, or respected. He may express his sympathy to a friend who has lost a loved one, even if he never met the deceased person.

The simplest statements are the most eloquent. A gentleman might write, "I considered Harold a valuable and trusted friend. I will miss him very much." To comfort a friend he might write, "I know Harold's loss is a great blow to you. My thoughts are with you in this difficult time."

A gentleman never says, "Please let me know if there is anything I can do," leaving it up to the grieving person to ask for help. Instead he offers to supply a meal for the family, to run an errand, or to watch the house while the family is away.

How to Write a
Thank-You Note

A gentleman knows that it is never wrong to write a thank-you note for any kindness that he has received—whether it is a birthday gift, dinner at a restaurant, a cocktail party in a friend's home, a weekend stay in a friend's beach house, or a ride to the garage to pick up his car. In every case, however, he keeps his thank-you brief and to the point. He specifically mentions the kindness he has received. ("The mauve sweater is just exactly what I'd been wanting." "Dinner was great. I'm so very fond of zucchini casserole." "I don't know how I'd ever have made it to work if you hadn't given me a lift to the Auto Outlet.")

An e-mail message, no matter how heartfelt, does not adequately express his gratitude. A handwritten note, no matter how brief, is the only gentlemanly option.

Net Worth

The vast world of the social network is a part of almost every gentleman's life. Even though traditional good taste still demands that he send along a handwritten note to mark any of life's highly ceremonial or deeply solemn occasions, such as the wedding of a friend or the death of the loved one of a friend, a gentleman can still incorporate e-mailing into his well-mannered life.

As a quick rule of thumb, a gentleman finds it appropriate to send an e-mail to handle any communication that he might otherwise take care of by means of a phone call. For example, an e-mail saying "Thanks for drinks last night. It was fun being with you," or "Thanks for the ride to the airport. You're a lifesaver," is every bit as thoughtful as—and perhaps more thoughtful than—a message left in voice mail. A brief, to-the-point e-mail is also a correct response to any invitation that was itself sent via the Internet.

A gentleman may also choose to express his joy upon the news of a happy occasion or his sadness at a friend's loss by sending a brief, but scrupulously worded, e-mail. He may say, "So glad to hear about the impending nuptials" or "I've just heard about your mother's death. Please know you are in my thoughts." Once again, in such cases, an e-mail may actually trump a phone call, since it does not intrude into the life of a friend who may either be tied up in wedding plans or disconcerted with grief.

In such instances, however, a gentleman knows that the e-mail does not complete his to-do list. He must follow up with a hand-written note, as soon as he possibly can, lest it appear that he is being dismissive of his friend's joy or sadness.

In no case may Twitter, Facebook or any of the more public social networks be used to respond to any of life's more solemn occasions. A gentleman would never run the risk of being deemed so impersonal, much less the risk of seeing his private thoughts shared with the teeming masses.

How to Make a Complaint

There are times when a gentleman is perfectly justified in lodging a complaint. If he has received poor service, if he has been treated rudely, or if he has been the target of an undeserved affront, he has every right to make his displeasure known—not only for the sake of his bruised feelings, but also in hopes that the unpleasantness will not occur again.

A gentleman knows, however, that it is useless to make a complaint unless it is made to the right person. For instance, if a gentleman has received inferior service in a restaurant, he does not waste his breath complaining directly to the server, who may feel no compulsion to amend his or her behavior. Instead, a gentleman expresses his concern to the manager or owner of the establishment. If he has the opportunity, he makes his complaint in person; otherwise, he makes a telephone call or he puts his concerns in writing.

When a gentleman makes a complaint, he specifically describes the reasons for his displeasure. He does not make threats. If he is poorly served at a restaurant or at any other establishment, he may choose to take his business elsewhere.

A gentleman recognizes that other people's beliefs are valid. He argues only over an issue that could save a life.

———

A gentleman never claims to have seen a movie he has not seen or to have read a book about which he has only read reviews. He knows how to say, "I haven't read [or seen] that yet, but from what I hear about it, it sounds very interesting. What did you think?"

———

A gentleman knows that "please" and "thank you" are still the magic words.

———

If a gentleman is in financial distress, he does not bore other people with the details. If he is flush, he leaves that out of the conversation, too.

Even if other people in the room are speaking in a foreign language, a gentleman is careful not to talk about them. He may not be able to speak Russian, but that does not mean the Russians are not fluent in English.

———

A gentleman never asks a woman if she is pregnant. He never asks, "Haven't you had that baby yet?"

———

A gentleman thinks before he speaks.

Chapter Five

A GENTLEMAN GIVES A PARTY

A gentleman does not give BYOB parties.

————

Whenever he can avoid it, a gentleman does not extend last-minute invitations. He knows that ninety minutes before the start of his party is too late to invite anybody to anything.

————

A gentleman does not answer the phone during dinner; he does not even bring his cell phone to the table. If he receives a call while he is entertaining, he leaves the table in order to answer it and politely asks the caller if he may return the call later.

The Heart of Hosting

When he acts as host—in his own home or in a restaurant—a gentleman does everything in his power to entertain his guests. He knows that his goal is to put them at ease, not to impress them. He feels no need to serve the most extravagant hors d'oeuvres possible; neither does he feel compelled to take guests to the most expensive restaurant in the city.

When his guests arrive, a gentleman greets them warmly and points them in the direction of food and drink. If he observes that a guest is not being included in the conversation, he introduces him or her to others and facilitates the conversation.

A gentleman host does not fret over broken glassware or scratches on the furniture. He accepts such irritations as a part of entertaining.

A gentleman makes sure that his invitation, whether delivered by telephone or by mail—or, in the most casual of circumstances, by e-mail—provides all the necessary information. He gives the time, the date, and the location. He also lets people know what they are expected to wear.

————

Should a guest arrive with an unexpected bottle of wine, and if it does not complement the menu he has planned, a gentleman simply says, "Thank you, Gloria. You are so thoughtful, and I love pinot noir. I'm certainly going to look forward to enjoying this soon."

————

If a guest offers to bring the wine or to help in some other way with the dinner menu, a gentleman may either accept or decline the offer. Either way, he says, "Thank you," and means it.

Should a guest arrive with a bowl of dip, or even a full-fledged casserole, a gentleman must find some way to serve it, even if it does not go well with the Dover sole he has so lovingly prepared.

————

A gentleman feels no need to write a thank-you note for any gift a guest has brought to him, provided it is clear the gift is intended as a thank-you to him for hosting the party.

How to Set Up a Bar

A gentleman does not stock his bar in order to impress people. He stocks his bar with the libations people actually want to drink. For even the largest, most eclectic group, a choice of scotch, vodka, gin, white wine, red wine, and in the South, bourbon will suffice. What is more, his guests will find themselves much less confused.

If he is concerned that dribbles of red wine will permanently stain his light-colored carpet, he serves only white.

In every case, a gentleman makes sure to have ample ice, and he offers a variety of mixers, not just for the pleasure of his drinking friends, but out of consideration for his nondrinking guests, as well. Quality, a gentleman knows, is always more important than quirkiness.

A gentleman knows that his bar is never complete without sliced limes and lemons, a jigger, a stirrer, and a tall stack of neatly pressed cotton cocktail napkins (or at the very least, paper napkins of the best quality he can afford) and a generous supply of glasses.

Should he run low on ice, a gentleman feels free to ask one of his guests to make an ice run. The gentleman provides the money for the ice, of course, giving it to the guest before he leaves the party. (A gentleman never leaves his own party, except in a dire emergency.)

A gentleman knows that, as a general rule, it is safest to have at least five pounds of ice on hand for every guest at a cocktail party. That quantity may seem exorbitant, but—especially on a warm evening—a gentleman will probably discover that there are very few cubes left in his cooler once the last guest has headed for home.

When liquor is being served, a gentleman host is always alert to the possibility that some guests may overindulge. In such cases he does not allow them to drive. He arranges for them to be driven home by a sober friend, or he calls a cab and, if necessary, pays for it himself. If he feels he must take away a guest's car keys, he does so.

––––––––

If a gentleman wants his guests to leave, he puts the liquor away.

––––––––

If he is not serving liquor and he finds that his friends are lingering a bit too late over their after-dinner coffee, a gentleman simply says, "It's been so much fun having you all here with me tonight. But tomorrow is an early morning for me. I hope we can get together again really soon."

Help Wanted

If a gentleman feels he will need assistance in throwing a party, particularly if it is a large gathering, or if he is less than confident in his skills behind the bar or in the kitchen, he engages the services of a bartender, a caterer, or both.

Before hiring help for a party, a gentleman seeks the advice of friends whose hosting skills he respects. If he is inexperienced when it comes to throwing parties, he is not ashamed to ask how much he should expect to pay for top-flight service. He knows it is wise to contact the bartender or caterer well ahead of time since the best people in those professions are often fully booked, especially during the holidays. He also knows that he may need to make more than one call in order to find servers who fit his budget.

In his consultations with a potential caterer or bartender, a gentleman makes it clear how many people he is inviting to his party, offers an idea as to the menu he would like to serve, and is careful to outline the service he expects. For instance, he makes it clear whether he wants the servers to pass drinks or hors d'oeuvres, or whether he merely expects them to serve from behind the bar or set out the buffet. He lets them know what time he expects them to arrive and how long the party will last. He makes sure they understand whether he expects them to bring the ice or whether he will be providing it himself.

In his first conversation with a caterer or a bartender, a gentleman asks, straightforwardly, how much he will be charged and if their services are available for the date of his event. If the estimate is beyond his budget, or if he is not happy with the menu suggestions he is offered, he says, "Thank you so much, but this isn't quite what I had in mind. Maybe we can work together another time."

Once he has engaged the services of a caterer, he depends on the caterer for advice. He will quickly learn that an experienced, well-connected caterer can be invaluable. He will also find that caterers can provide their own serving dishes and will even engage and supervise the bartenders. In every circumstance, a gentleman can expect the caterers to stay until the established closing time for the party and to leave his home (especially his kitchen) cleaner than it was when they arrived.

If he is paying a set fee to his bartenders or his caterer, he does not tip them. If he wishes to do so, he may tip any servers who have come to assist the caterer, but he does not permit them to set out tip jars at a party in his home.

A gentleman makes sure to exchange cell phone numbers with the bartenders and the caterer, in case he needs answers to last-minute questions or should emergencies arise.

A gentleman host uses his good china. If a piece is broken accidentally, he does not make a scene; neither does he accept a guest's offer to pay for its replacement.

————

A gentleman sometimes discovers that he has made the mistake of inviting ill-mannered people into his home. He does not attempt to reform such people's behavior. Instead, he does not invite them back again.

————

A gentleman does not make excuses for his misbehaving guests. He may wish, however, to offer an apology to an offended guest by saying, "Tom, it was so good to see you last night. I'm sorry Millicent was so argumentative."

How to Seat a Table

If a gentleman entertains—whether in his home or in a public place—the moment will come when he will be expected to "seat" a table. At that moment he, as a host, will be asked to decide where each of his guests will sit during the meal ahead of them. A gentleman takes this obligation seriously, knowing that his decision will make or break the evening. He attempts to seat compatible guests beside each other, but he never seats a couple—whether they are married, a long-standing couple, or on a first date—side by side. His goal is to create a mix of guests who will ask each other questions, generating lively conversation.

If there is a guest of honor, that person is always given the best seat. At a banquet, for example, the honored guest is given the seat with the best view of the room. In a private home, the guest of honor is seated at the host's right hand or, better yet, between two particularly congenial guests.

Meanwhile, a gentleman-host reserves for himself the least desirable seat. For instance, at a formal dinner where there are to be speeches, the host takes the seat with the poorest view of the podium. His compensatory reward comes from watching the happy faces of his handsomely entertained guests.

If a gentleman is giving an extremely intimate dinner party—for only one or two guests—he may ask his guests to join him in the kitchen as he finishes the dinner preparations. If his kitchen is small, they may stand in the doorway so that he can join in the conversation.

HOW TO SET A DINNER TABLE

A gentleman knows how to set an elegant, if rudimentary, dinner table. The basic equipment is arranged in this manner:

When Salad is served as a First Course

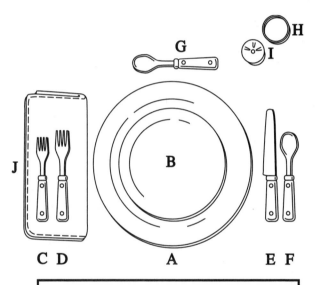

A. Dinner Plate	F. Teaspoon
B. Salad Plate	G. Dessert spoon*
C. Salad Fork	H. Water Glass
D. Dinner Fork	I. Wine Goblet
E. Dinner Knife	J. Napkin

The dessert utensil can be a fork if appropriate.

When Salad is Served along with the entrée

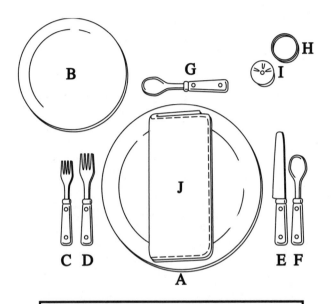

A. Dinner Plate	F. Teaspoon
B. Salad Plate	G. Dessert spoon*
C. Salad Fork	H. Water Glass
D. Dinner Fork	I. Wine Goblet
E. Dinner Knife	J. Napkin

The dessert utensil can be a fork if appropriate.

How to Serve Dinner

Before a gentleman's guests arrive, he sets out the dinner plates, flatware, and glasses on the table. Once the guests have chatted for a bit and have perhaps had a drink of some sort, he suggests that they proceed to the table. Thereafter, the procedure is as follows:

1. The guests take their places.
2. If a gentleman is serving a salad, he places the salad plates directly on the dinner plates (which have already been set).
3. When the guests have finished their salads, a gentleman removes the salad plates. If he plans to serve the dinner plates in the kitchen, he takes them away at the same time.
4. A gentleman either serves the dinner plates in the kitchen or brings the main course and its side dishes to the table, where the guests serve themselves.
5. When guests have finished the main course, with second helpings if they are offered, a gentleman takes away the dinner plates, along with the dinner forks and knives.
6. A gentleman serves dessert. If he has not already placed the dessert forks or spoons on the table, he may bring them out with the dessert itself. If there is coffee, he serves it now.

If the dinner conversation continues after the guests have finished their desserts, a gentleman takes the empty plates away and pours more coffee. He never rushes his friends to leave the table after a satisfying meal.

———

If a gentleman prefers to prepare the dinner himself, he tells his guests and graciously declines their offers for help. If he would like their assistance, however, he accepts their offers. If an offer is not made, he may still ask for help in small chores, such as opening the wine or filling the glasses with ice.

———

If a guest offers to help clean up after the party, a gentleman may either accept or decline the offer. However, he has no reason to expect that such an offer will be made. From start to finish, hosting a party is a one-man job.

———

As his guests depart, a gentleman sees each one of them to the door and watches until they reach the elevator, the stairs, or the driveway.

Chapter Six

A GENTLEMAN GOES TO A PARTY

A gentleman considers any invitation an act of generosity and kindness. He accepts or declines it as promptly and as graciously as possible.

————

When a gentleman receives a number of invitations for the same date, via voice mail or e-mail, he accepts the first one. A gentleman knows it is rude to weigh one invitation against another.

————

A gentleman *never* waits for something better to turn up.

If a gentleman finds that his schedule will allow him to stop in at more than one event on the same day or evening, he does so. He explains to his host or hostess ahead of time, however, that such will be the case. If he is invited to a dinner party and will not be able to stay for the actual dinner, he is scrupulous in making his intentions clear.

———

Unless he foresees an unavoidable scheduling conflict—or unless he finds the company of his host or hostess, or the company of their friends, truly unbearable—a gentleman does not turn down invitations. (The fact that a friend is boring does not constitute "unbearable" behavior.)

———

A gentleman does not
crash parties.

If prior experience has taught a gentleman to expect unpleasant behavior, or even illegal behavior (such as drinking and driving or drug use), on the part of his host or hostess, or their usual group of friends, he declines their invitation politely, saying, "I wish I could join you, Morris, but I already have an engagement that evening." A gentleman knows that this is the whitest lie possible. Even if he merely plans to stay home and watch a rented movie, that still constitutes an "engagement."

———

A gentleman does not take a date to a party unless he is certain he is expected to do so. If his invitation is not addressed to him "and guest," he does not have the license to bring an extra person along.

How to Respond to an Invitation

A gentleman wastes no time in responding to an invitation. If he sees the letters RSVP (an abbreviation for the French equivalent of "Please reply") at the bottom of a written invitation, he is obligated to respond, either by telephone or in writing. An RSVP requires that he reply, even if he does not plan to attend the event in question. If the directive is "Regrets only," he need inform his host or hostess only if he does *not* plan to show up. A gentleman understands that it is vastly inconsiderate for him not to make his intentions known.

If a gentleman must decline an invitation, he gives a straightforward reason for doing so. "I have a prior engagement," "I will have guests from out of town," and "I will be away on vacation" are all perfectly acceptable explanations.

A gentleman does not lay down conditions for his accepting an invitation. He does not ask, "What will you be serving?" or "Who else is going to be there?" He accepts the invitation gladly and proves to himself that because he is a gentleman, he can have a good time in any company, at any time.

If a gentleman has been invited to a party via e-mail, he may either respond in kind or pick up the telephone and say, "Hello, Pete. I got your invitation for eight o'clock on Friday. I'm looking forward to being there," or "Hello, Patricia. I got your invitation for Friday. I wish I could be there, but I'm going to be in Minneapolis." A voice-mail message will usually suffice as a reply to any invitation received via telephone or e-mail. Because voice-mail services sometimes malfunction, however, a gentleman will feel more at ease if he speaks directly to his host or hostess.

Whenever he accepts an invitation in writing, by phone, or by e-mail, a gentleman makes it clear that he knows what time he is expected to arrive and where he is expected to be. In his response he says, "I can't wait to see you at 7:30 on Saturday, at your place."

When a gentleman discovers that he can attend a party for which he has already refused an invitation, he calls his host or hostess and asks whether he may attend.

———

If a gentleman discovers that he must decline an invitation that he has already accepted, he promptly lets his host or hostess know. He gives a frank description of the reasons for his change of plan and offers a sincere apology.

COAT CHECK

A gentleman understands the dress code provided on his party invitation. "Casual" varies with the season: shorts and a polo shirt for summer, jeans and a sweater for winter. "Business casual" suggests an open shirt and a sports jacket. "Semiformal" requires a dark suit and tie. "Black tie" dictates a dinner jacket and its necessary accoutrements: a vest or cummerbund, cufflinks and studs, a good white shirt, and brightly polished black shoes. "White tie" demands the gentleman's ultimate regalia, complete with tailcoat and patent leather dancing shoes.

Nevertheless, confusion may persist. The chart on the next page offers some guidance.

A GUIDE TO THE LANGUAGE OF THE DRESS CODE

If the Invitation Says . . .	A Gentleman Wears . . .
Black Tie	dinner clothes (tuxedo)
White Tie	evening clothes ("white tie and tails")
Black Tie Optional	a tuxedo or dark suit
Semiformal	a dark suit
Festive Informal	a suit and brightly colored tie
Cocktail Attire	a dark suit or dressy sports coat
Business Attire	a suit and tie
Business Casual	a sports coat; tie is optional
Casual Chic	a sports coat or sweater and slacks
Casual	jeans, slacks, or shorts

When a gentleman responds to any invitation, if he is not certain as to the dress code for the occasion, he simply asks, "What do you think the other guys will be wearing?"

———

A gentleman is never the last to leave a party. Neither, if he can possibly help it, is he the first to arrive.

———

A gentleman knows to start with the fork on the outside. If the salad fork is in the wrong place, he does not make a scene.

———

Once a gentleman's dinner knife has been dirtied, he rests it on the edge of his dinner plate. He never lets it touch the tablecloth.

Glad to Be Included

A gentleman knows that accepting an invitation is like signing a business contract. His host or hostess promises to entertain the guests, and he agrees to do his part to make the event a success.

He arrives on time—not early and not more than fifteen minutes late, especially if a meal is being served. (For a more flexibly structured event such as a cocktail party, a birthday party, or a gathering around the pool, scheduled over the course of three hours, he may arrive an hour or so into the festivities. If the invitation is for seven to ten o'clock, however, he does not wait until 9:45 to make his appearance.) He participates in the activities that have been planned, and he makes pleasant conversation with the other guests. He does not gorge himself at the dinner table, although he takes a second helping when it is offered. He does not overindulge at the bar.

When the party is winding down, he exits with efficient grace. He thanks his host or hostess and says good-bye to any new friends he may have made.

A gentleman does not use his host's or hostess's home phone or cell phone, without first asking permission.

———

At a party a gentleman never spends all his time talking to one person. He is always excited to meet as many people as possible, and he assumes that a great many people will enjoy meeting him, too.

———

A gentleman uses a coaster.

———

A gentleman feels free to use the hand towel in the powder room. That is why it has been placed out on the counter.

When faced with a plate of long pasta—such as spaghetti, linguine, or fettuccine—a gentleman resists every temptation to chop it up with his knife and fork. Instead, he twirls a manageable mouthful around the tines of his fork and, with the help of his spoon, transfers it to his mouth.

———

A gentleman asks for seconds when they are offered. If he has any good sense, however, he watches to see whether other guests are following suit. He knows it is the worst possible form to expect his fellow diners, once they have obviously finished eating, to wait while he works his way through an extra helping of beef Stroganoff.

When to Take a Gift

When a gentleman is invited to another person's home—for dinner, a holiday party, or an overnight visit—he takes a gift. For a dinner party, he takes a bouquet of flowers or a bottle of wine (unchilled, so that the host or hostess knows that it is a *gift* and is not intended to accompany dinner). For a holiday party, he takes a jar of mustard, some jam, a bottle of good whiskey, a tin of nuts, or a bag of coffee beans. If he is invited for a more extended stay—a single night or longer—a gentleman takes a more substantial gift, such as cloth cocktail napkins, an extra corkscrew, an interesting book, or a useful kitchen gadget.

A gentleman always presents his gift directly to his host or hostess. If a gentleman takes a gift to a party, unless it is a baby or wedding shower, he does not assume that it will be opened in his presence.

How to Make a Toast

Over the course of his life, a gentleman will probably be invited to any number of wedding receptions, anniversary dinners, birthday parties, and other events. At some time, almost inevitably, he will be asked to make a toast, and if he is asked, he must not refuse. However, he need not attempt to give an after-dinner speech or perform a comedy routine. His tribute may be something as simple as "Joe, I'm proud to call you my friend." He may choose to share some memory of his friendship with the honoree, or if he is confident of his skill as a humorist, he may toss off a lighthearted quip. In no case does he attempt to embarrass the guest of honor. Neither does he ramble on at any length. A gentleman remembers that because toasts usually come late in the evening, the wisest course is always to be succinct.

If a toast is being made, a gentleman, even if he is a teetotaler, always raises his glass. He never toasts with an empty glass. Even a glass of water, raised in the right spirit, expresses a wish for good luck.

After a toast has been made, a gentleman clinks his glass against any other glass that is extended toward his own.

A gentleman has never been seated beside a boring person at dinner. Neither has he ever been seated beside a person who has been bored.

———

A gentleman may not be able to dance a samba, but he should be capable of a box step, which is almost like not dancing at all.

When to Send a
Thank-You Note

A gentleman always sends a thank-you note. Whether he brought flowers or a casserole to a potluck dinner, he is still grateful. Even if he brings a bottle of wine, he still writes a note. (The flowers say, "Thank you for inviting me." The note says, "Thank you, I had a good time." It is not the same thing.) If he brought flowers or wine, the note does not have to be sent immediately. If the evening was boring, or if he left early, he can always say something like, "I had such fun pausing with you before the marathon of yet another busy weekend." Or he can say, "Dinner was so good, I tried a little bit of everything."

He does not expect his host or hostess to reply to a thank-you note.

Unless he is asked to do so, a gentleman does not operate another person's sound system. Neither does he touch another person's CDs.

———

If a gentleman arrives at a private party and discovers that valet parking has been provided, he pulls into line and waits his turn. When he pulls up to the door of the house, he allows the parking attendant to open the car doors–both for the gentleman's guests and for the gentleman himself. The gentleman does not forget to leave the keys in the ignition. He makes sure to have his tip money ready at the end of the evening.

———

When a gentleman chooses not to drink wine, he feels perfectly confident in telling his host, "No, thank you. I'll just have some water [or some iced tea or some soda]."

If a gentleman guest breaks a piece of china or glassware when being entertained at another person's home (and it *does* happen—not all gentlemen are graceful), he apologizes. Instead of offering to pay for its replacement, however, he does his best to replace the broken item itself.

———

If a gentleman discovers a raspberry seed or some other obstruction lodged between his teeth, he excuses himself and heads for the restroom.

———

If a gentleman is in need of a toothpick, he uses it, but only as quickly and deftly as possible. He does not chew on it, once its work is done.

———

When a gentleman is offered a name tag, he puts it on.

Chapter Seven

A GENTLEMAN AND HIS FRIENDS

A gentleman never gets so big that he can feel free to say or do things that make other people feel small.

———

A gentleman does not lend more money than he can afford to spare. He does not borrow more money than he can afford to pay back.

———

If a gentleman says he will call, he lives up to his word.

———

A gentleman is perfectly willing to accept no for an answer—the *first* time he hears it.

How to Shake Hands

A gentleman feels free to shake hands with anyone to whom he is introduced, or with any acquaintance he encounters in a social situation, whether at a party, in a theater lobby, or in an aisle at church. However, a gentleman does respect certain guidelines. When he is introduced to an older person or to a dignitary, a gentleman does not extend his hand first. Instead, he waits until a handshake is offered. Then he firmly grasps the extended hand, just below the knuckles, and gives it a couple of modest pumps. He uses a light, painless grip and lets go immediately after the handshake is finished.

A gentleman never extends his hand to a woman first. It is always her prerogative to decide if she wishes to shake hands. In any case, when shaking hands with a woman, a gentleman is wise to give her hand a quick, gentle press rather than a full-fledged up-and-down pump. If a lady does not extend her hand, a gentleman simply nods his head as a gesture of greeting.

When a young boy is introduced to him, a gentleman initiates the handshake. When a young girl is introduced to him, he simply says, "Hello, Mary Ann, it's nice to meet you."

A gentleman never refuses to shake a hand that is extended to him. Such a refusal is the most blatant insult possible in the business or the social world.

Whenever possible, a gentleman stays away from sore subjects.

———————

In matters of politics or religion, a gentleman does not assume that everyone believes what he believes.

The Art of the Social Kiss

A gentleman knows that a social kiss is not an erotic experience. It expresses the mildest sort of affection. It happens quickly and means hardly more than a handshake. A social kiss is shared only among people who are already friends. It is never offered in a business situation.

A gentleman always waits for the woman to initiate a social kiss. If she leans toward him, he turns his cheek toward her lips, and she graces him with a light, brushing kiss. She does not linger in giving the kiss. Neither does he dawdle in accepting it. He may place one hand on her shoulder.

If a woman's lipstick leaves a smudge on a gentleman's face, he does not wipe it away in her presence. Instead, he bears it, even if briefly, as a badge of honor, wiping it away later with his handkerchief.

A gentleman does not smooch, make out, or engage in any other intimate behavior in a public place.

————

When a gentleman is in the company of a woman—whether she is his mother, his wife, his date, his boss, or his friend—and they are walking through a crowded room, he walks slightly behind her.

————

If a gentleman recognizes friends or acquaintances at other tables in a restaurant, he feels free to greet them, but only in the least intrusive way possible. He may stop by their table to greet them cordially, but he does not interrupt their dinner or their conversation for long.

————

If friends stand up to greet him when he stops by their table, a gentleman urges them immediately to return to their seats.

Hold the Sauce

Any gentleman may have friends who do not drink alcohol. Whatever the reason for that choice—religious belief, an addiction, or other health concerns—a gentleman respects it. He does not pressure anyone to drink; neither does he ask probing questions. When he is serving as a host, in his own home or in a restaurant, he makes certain that his nondrinking friends have plenty of appealing nonalcoholic options.

If a gentleman chooses not to drink alcohol, he does not impose that decision on other people. If he is offered a cocktail, he may say, "Thanks, but I don't drink alcohol. I'd like a soda or some sparkling water—whatever you have handy." He offers no further explanation.

The Gift of Giving

A gentleman knows that it is a very dangerous thing to ask another person, "What do you want for Christmas?" At best, the answer will be, "I don't know—surprise me." At worst, it will be something a gentleman cannot provide. In either case, the answer will probably not be what the gentleman wants to hear. When he is planning to buy a gift for a friend or loved one, his best option will be to watch carefully and listen closely, in hopes of picking up helpful hints.

Whenever he plans to buy a gift, he goes shopping well ahead of time. He always does his best to avoid a last-minute panic, which almost inevitably leads to acts of desperation and gift-giving disasters.

PACKAGE DEALS:

Failsafe Suggestions for Picking the Perfect Present

Birthdays

For a Lady Friend: flowers, a picture
frame, a new best seller, dinner or lunch
at a favorite restaurant

For a Gentleman Friend: a bottle of good
whiskey or wine, tickets to an upcoming
sports event, drinks and/or lunch or
dinner at a favorite bar or restaurant, a
best-selling CD

For His Fiancée: flowers, a piece of
jewelry (a family heirloom, if possible), a
framed photograph of the two of them,
candlelight dinner (preferably prepared
by the gentleman himself)

For His Wife: breakfast in bed, dinner
at a fine restaurant, jewelry, lingerie
(provided the gentleman is confident he
knows her size and her favorite colors)

For His Mother: Sunday lunch or
Saturday brunch, flowers, a simple
article of clothing (such as a sweater,
scarf, or gloves), tickets to an upcoming
concert

For His Father: lunch for just the two of them, sporting equipment (such as tennis balls or golf balls), tickets to a sporting event, cuff links, a DVD of a favorite movie

For His Administrative Assistant: flowers, if his assistant is a woman; a book, a DVD, or a CD, if the assistant is a man (almost anything else is too personal)

Weddings

For Friends: wine glasses, barware, silver picture frame, serving tray, salad bowl with serving pieces, a piece of the china or flatware for which they have registered

For Business Acquaintances or His Friend's Children: a piece of their chosen china or flatware

For His Attendants, If He Is the Groom: cuff links, book, money clip

Housewarmings: a bottle of good wine or liquor, barware, cloth cocktail napkins, picture frame, small serving bowl or serving tray

Anniversaries

For His Wife: dinner at an intimate restaurant, a night on the town (including tickets to the theater or a concert), flowers, jewelry, lingerie, or a luxurious blouse

For His Parents: gift certificate for dinner, tickets to a show or movie, framed photograph of their children, grandchildren, or pet

Valentine's Day: flowers, candy, a romantic dinner

Bar or Bat Mitzvahs: check, gift certificate to a good bookstore, donation to a social-service agency in the bar or bat mitzvah's honor

Baptisms or Christenings: silver rattle, monogrammed bed pillow (for a girl), engraved pewter cup (for a boy), monogrammed picture frame, savings bond

Unless he is invited to a friend's birthday party, a gentleman feels comfortable simply sending a card. He does his best to keep a record of his friends' birthdays so his cards can go out on time.

———

Unless he is invited to a party in their honor, a gentleman does not feel compelled to give anniversary gifts to friends who are not related to him.

———

A gentleman may learn that a bride and groom, a bar or bat mitzvah, or the honorees at a birthday or anniversary gathering, have asked that donations be sent to a specific charitable organization, in lieu of gifts. If that is the expressed desire of the honorees, a gentleman respects their wishes.

When purchasing a gift for his wife or sweetheart, especially if it is a gift for Valentine's Day, a birthday, or an anniversary, a gentleman never goes shopping in the hardware or housewares department. On such occasions, he knows, a gift with an electrical cord attached is never appropriate.

———

Unless he is giving a gift to a young person, about whose taste and hobbies he has no clue, a gentleman avoids giving a gift certificate, a phone card, or a purchase card, except as a very last resort.

The Second Time Around

From time to time, a gentleman may receive a gift that he cannot use—either because it is a duplicate of something he already has or because it simply does not suit his taste. In such cases, if a gentleman is certain the gift will be appropriate for another person, he feels perfectly free to "re-gift" it, provided he takes certain precautions:

- He always makes sure to rewrap the gift in fresh paper.
- He makes sure to remove any enclosure card that might indicate the gift is being recycled.
- He does not "re-gift" among his circle of close friends or among family members. (If he is wise, he will not even "re-gift" among friends or acquaintances who live in the same city.)
- He waits a considerable time (six months or even as long as a year) before passing a gift along.

If a gentleman receives a gift that he cannot, or knows he will not, use, he is especially careful in writing his thank-you note. For example, he does not promise to wear a sweater of a color that does not flatter him; neither does he promise that he will prominently display a pseudo-vintage lava lamp (unless that pseudo-vintage lava lamp actually suits his décor). Instead, he says, "The puce turtleneck looks like just the right thing for those cold winter nights," or "The lamp reminds me of those parties we went to back in Millersville. Where do you find such amazing, unique gifts?"

When to Send Flowers

A gentleman feels free to send flowers to mark almost any occasion, happy or sad. Flowers may celebrate an anniversary, a birthday, a holiday, a promotion, the birth of a baby, or any other joyful moment in life. They are the perfect means of thanking a host or hostess, and they may be sent either before or after the party. On the other hand, flowers may also be sent to comfort a grieving family or to brighten a sick person's room. They may be sent to say "I'm sorry" when a gentleman has been guilty of an unintentional affront.

At the same time, a gentleman knows that there are a few occasions when flowers—or at least certain types of flowers—are not the right gesture. If a mourning family has asked that no flowers be sent to a funeral, a gentleman sends none. Before sending flowers to a funeral service or to a family in mourning, a gentleman always checks to make sure a gift of flowers is appropriate in the family's religious tradition. (It is not appropriate, for example, to send flowers to a Jewish family while they are sitting shiva.)

If a gentleman is not accustomed to sending flowers, he asks his friends to recommend the name of a reputable, affordable florist. (A gentleman makes it clear what is "affordable" for him by stating forthrightly, "I'd like to spend about fifty dollars" or whatever amount he truly can afford to spend.) When calling the florist, he describes the occasion for which he is sending the flowers and says, "I'd like to send something in the fifty-dollar range."

He does not send flowers to his administrative assistant—or to any other coworker—at her home. Instead he has an arrangement of cut flowers or, better yet, a hardy green plant delivered to her desk.

Finally, a gentleman knows that unless a woman is a grandmother of the bride, he never sends a corsage.

When there is a woman on the premises—or if there is any likelihood a woman will arrive soon—a gentleman always puts the toilet seat down.

————

In the morning, a gentleman always offers to get up and make the coffee.

————

A gentleman does not make phone calls to anyone during the time when he knows they will be dining.

————

A gentleman never tells jokes that may embarrass other people, even if those other people are not in the room.

————

A gentleman is not afraid to carry breath mints. Neither is he reluctant to offer them to other people.

How to Be a Houseguest

As a guest in a private home, a gentleman treats his host's furniture and other belongings with the greatest care, even more carefully than if they were his own.

If there are servants and some special service is done for him, or if he stays any great length of time, he shows his gratitude by leaving a thank-you tip.

In every case, a gentleman attempts to fit into the household routine. He rises and retires according to the household schedule. He eats what is served and does not complain. (If he has food allergies or other dietary restrictions, he makes sure his host or hostess is aware of them well ahead of time.) He makes his bed in the morning, and he disposes of damp towels as he is instructed.

Most important, he sticks to his arrival and departure plans. When his visit is over, he checks his room to make sure he has packed all his belongings. He leaves nothing but pleasant memories behind.

A Gentleman and His Unmarried Friends

A gentleman may have many friends and acquaintances who live together in nontraditional relationships. If a gentleman decides to make these people a part of his life, he accepts them as they are, recognizing that their private life is their business and no one else's. If he does not approve of their behavior, he does not preach to them. Instead, he associates with them as seldom as possible.

In no case does he mention their relationship when introducing them to other people. For example, a gentleman does not say, "This is Mary Brown, and this is her live-in boyfriend [or "her significant other" or "the father of her child"], Sam Jones." Instead, he says, "I'd like you to meet my friends Mary Brown and Sam Jones."

If the couple feels the need to provide any further details about their living arrangement, they may do so, although in most cases they will be telling people more than they really need or want to know.

In written correspondence with Mary and Sam, a gentleman addresses the envelope to "Ms. Mary Brown and Mr. Sam Jones." Similarly, a letter to his friends Bob and Keith would be addressed to "Mr. Bob Grainger and Mr. Keith Harris." And a letter to his friends Kate and Helen would go to "Ms. Helen Thompson and Ms. Kate Williams," listing them in alphabetical order.

A gentleman is patient with his friends and tolerant of their individual quirks. He knows that a good friend, no matter how quirky, is worth holding close to his heart for life.

A Gentleman and His Divorced Friends

A gentleman regrets seeing any loving relationship break up, especially if he considers both persons to be his friends. However, his regret is for *their* pain, not for his own. He does not take sides in their marital strife; he does not carry tales back and forth between the opposing camps.

If his friends are recently divorced, a gentleman does his best not to put them in situations—a small dinner party, for example—where they will be forced to encounter each other. He tries to maintain communication with both parties, but he understands that he is now friends with *two people*, not with a couple. Maintaining these friendships may require twice as much effort—and twice as much time.

After a reasonable amount of time has passed, a gentleman may feel free to include both friends in the same event, especially when a good many other people are involved. To forestall any anxiety, though, he is thoughtful enough to make sure both parties are informed ahead of time. He also makes sure that his guest list includes other single people so that the divorced person does not feel like a fifth wheel.

A gentleman may say to Betsy, formerly married to Tom, "It's going to be fun, Betsy. I've invited Jim and Marcia, and Bob, Jim, Gloria, Ted, and Vivian. I'm going to ask Tom, too."

Because a gentleman's friends are well-mannered

people, they would never ask him for such information ahead of time. However, a gentleman understands if, given the circumstances, they choose to decline his invitation. Only in such extraordinary circumstances, after all, would a well-mannered person ever decline.

———

A gentleman never attempts to make a last-minute date. But if a couple of good tickets fall into his hands by happenstance, he does not neglect the opportunity to share them with someone whose company he enjoys.

———

A gentleman breaks a date only for reasons of sickness, death, or natural disaster. If he must cancel his plans, he does so with as much warning as possible.

———

Unless he has absolutely no other alternative, a gentleman never breaks a date by leaving a voice-mail message or via e-mail. Unless he must cancel because of a last-minute emergency, he considers such behavior the coward's way out.

A Friend in Need

Although a gentleman is always wary about correcting the behavior of others, he may sometimes discover that even one of his dearest friends is given to unintentionally boorish behavior, awkward table manners, or poor grammar. He is scrupulously careful when attempting to help a friend improve his behavior.

Unless his friend's behavior—such as overly loud talking or conducting a cell phone conversation in a theater or a doctor's office—is causing immediate distress to others, a gentleman does not correct his friend in public. Instead, he waits until the two of them are alone. Perhaps while he and his friend are on their way home from a restaurant or dinner party where the friend's table manners have not been up to par, the gentleman can say, as directly as possible, "Pete, I noticed that you were drinking your coffee out of your saucer this evening. That's really not a very good thing to do." He does not say, "I caught you drinking coffee out of your saucer." Neither does he say, "That's not what nice people do."

A gentleman does not wait until a mountain of offenses has piled up before he gives his advice. Neither does he hand down broad, theatrical judgments, such as "You know, Pete, you really have just about the worst table manners I've ever seen." A gentleman knows that hurtful words are never helpful to anybody.

A gentleman takes care not to critique a friend's behavior too frequently, lest the friend feel that he is being constantly scrutinized. Ultimately, he knows that a good friend—even one with more than a few foibles—is to be treasured, not tormented.

And above all else, before he corrects another person on any point, a gentleman always makes sure that his own advice is correct. He would never want to lead a friend ever further astray or lead himself into self-inflicted embarrassment.

———

If a gentleman finds he must raise a sensitive subject with a friend or coworker, he does so in the kindest, but most direct, manner possible.

———

When a gentleman realizes that another gentleman has neglected to close his fly, he tells him about it, even in a crowded room.

———

When a gentleman realizes that his own fly is open, he zips up—on the spot, if convenient. Never does an open fly require an apology.

Chapter Eight

A GENTLEMAN GOES TO THE OFFICE

A gentleman may choose to carry work home from the office. He does not, however, assume that his fellow employees will do the same.

————

If a gentleman is in the position to supervise the work of other people in his office, he does not attempt to dictate. Instead, he directs.

————

A gentleman never writes personal letters on his business stationery.

The Manners of Voice Mail

A gentleman never assumes that anyone recognizes his voice when he leaves a voice-mail message, especially if he is making a business call. He speaks clearly, identifies himself, and leaves his phone number. Better yet, he speaks slowly and gives the number twice. In no case does a gentleman go on and on. He leaves a concise message and then gets on with his life.

When a gentleman's phone message is not returned in a timely fashion and a deadline is involved, he calls back and, if necessary, leaves a second message. At this point, it is the other person's responsibility to return the call.

If a gentleman receives a message that involves a deadline, he returns the message promptly.

If a gentleman works in an open office space, he remembers that others can overhear his conversations. He speaks in a quiet tone of voice. He does not shout across the office. Neither does he laugh raucously while others are busy working.

––––––––

If a gentleman is speaking on his cell phone and learns that he has a poor connection, he closes his office door or moves to an out-of-the-way part of the work space before raising his voice.

––––––––

If a gentleman borrows a pen from a fellow employee, he returns it promptly. He does not lose the cap.

A Gentleman and His Boss

Even in today's egalitarian society, a gentleman remembers that in some situations there still is a chain of command. He may be on a first-name basis with his employer, and they may enjoy an occasional golf game together, but he still remembers who is in charge in the office. He accepts his work assignments with good grace unless they are in some way repellent to him. If a gentleman feels the need to deny a request from his boss, he gives his reasons for doing so, with frankness and without delay.

In semisocial situations, such as having a casual drink after work, a gentleman accepts without resistance his boss's offer to pick up the tab—even if his boss is a woman. During the holidays, if his boss gives him a present, a gentleman accepts it and expresses his gratitude, perhaps by means of a simple thank-you note. He understands that his boss does not expect a gift in return. Such a present acknowledges a job well done; it does not suggest an exchange between friends.

A gentleman understands that a bonus check is a business gift and a pat on the back, pure and simple. The only acknowledgment it requires is a grateful "thank you." Should a gentleman receive a bonus, he does not mention it to his coworkers. If he learns that a fellow employee has also received a bonus, he does not ask, "How much did you get?"

When a gentleman is asked to take a message or accept a package for a fellow employee, he does so. He makes certain that he takes the message accurately, and he treats the package with care.

———

A gentleman always makes sure any delivery he accepts gets into the proper hands, perhaps sending an e-mail to the fellow employee saying, "Dear Jessica, I have a package for you in my office."

———

A gentleman does not lie on his résumé.

———

On a job interview, a gentleman dresses as he would for a day at the office. In that way he makes it clear that he understands the nature of the business.

———

When a gentleman resigns from his job, he does not burn bridges.

Because he does his homework before he shows up for an interview, a gentleman knows the office dress code well ahead of time.

———

After a job interview, a gentleman writes a thank-you note. He knows that an e-mail, no matter how hard he has labored in wording it, may seem like little more than an afterthought.

———

A gentleman always restocks the copy machine with paper.

———

If a gentleman drains the last cup of water from the water cooler, he makes sure a refill tank is installed. If a coworker asks a gentleman to help install a heavy refill tank, and if he is strong enough to provide real assistance, he does so.

The Staff of Life

A gentleman treats his administrative assistant and any other members of his staff with all the respect due a valued coworker and a fellow human being. He makes his expectations clearly known, and he readily expresses his gratitude for a job well done.

He is careful to keep the line clearly drawn between his personal and professional lives. If his level of trust is great enough, he may ask his assistant to make his bank deposit for him. However, unless this individual functions as the gentleman's personal assistant, he does not ask him or her to balance his checkbook or pay his bills. He may ask his assistant to set up a business lunch. He does not ask his assistant to set up a date.

He may give his assistant a gift on special occasions—such as a work anniversary, a birthday, or a holiday—but he is always wise to stick with flowers, a book, or some other impersonal item. He does not expect his assistant to give him a gift in return.

No matter how many years the two of them have worked together, and no matter how pressing the deadlines of their work, a gentleman does not neglect to tell his assistant, "Thank you." Even if he is only asking his assistant to make photocopies, he does not forget to say, "Please."

Unless he works in an extremely formal office, a gentleman and his assistant are usually on a first-name basis. If the assistant refers to him as "Mr. Saunders," the gentleman may wish to say, "Harriett [or Harry], I hope you'll go ahead and call me Bill." If the assistant persists in referring to him as "Mr. Saunders," the gentleman bows to the assistant's wishes.

A gentleman never asks a coworker, especially not one of his employees, to make the coffee. If he is a coffee drinker, he learns how to operate the coffeemaker himself.

———

If a gentleman drinks the last cup of coffee, he makes a new pot.

———

If a gentleman is the last to leave the office at the end of the day, he turns the coffee pot off.

———

If a gentleman realizes that he is going to be more than five minutes late for a business appointment, he telephones ahead or sends an e-mail or text message.

———

When leaving on a business trip with other colleagues, a gentleman shows up on time.

A Gentleman goes to the Office

If a gentleman is asked whether he wishes to share a hotel room while on a business trip, he makes his preference known. If company policy requires sharing rooms, he behaves courteously and considerately to his roommate.

———

On a business trip, a gentleman does not abuse the privileges of his expense account.

———

A gentleman does not mix business and pleasure, especially when it comes to travel. Unless his coworkers are doing the same, he does not bring his spouse or companion along on business trips.

———

When a gentleman is traveling for business, he is scrupulous in keeping track of his expenses and retains all necessary receipts.

Door Jam

A gentleman does his best, at all times, to tolerate the idiosyncrasies of others. In the office environment, however, he may find himself faced with a coworker whose behavior is not only irritating but also problematic to the office as a whole.

In some instances, a gentleman may attempt to handle such challenges on his own. For example, if a coworker is prone to barge into the gentleman's office while the gentleman is on the phone or is otherwise occupied, he simply says, "Nigel, I'm on the phone right now," or "Norvell, I'm on deadline for the PlastiCorp account. Now is not a good time for me to talk."

If a gentleman truly does not wish to be interrupted, he shuts his office door. If his office does not have a door, he feels free to post a notice saying, "No Interruptions, Please," or "On Deadline."

In virtually every office, however, there is at least one bullish employee who seems totally oblivious to personal boundaries. When dealing with this insensitive coworker, a gentleman must be as direct at possible, saying, "Frannie, when my office door is closed, it means I'm working and don't wish to be interrupted. I hope you will understand that." He may even wish to add, "If there's some business we urgently need to conduct, just send me an e-mail, and I'll get back to you as soon as possible."

If all else fails, a gentleman's last recourse is to ask his supervisor to discuss the problem with the unthinking fellow employee. The coworker may come away with bruised feelings, but the level of tension in the office will be greatly reduced.

When a gentleman entertains a business client, it is his responsibility to pick up the tab. If he knows that his client is likely to attempt to pay the bill, a gentleman makes sure ahead of time that the server will present him with the check and not ask, "Now which of you gets the bill?"

———

A gentleman realizes that a personal e-mail or a personal text message is like a personal phone call. He does not interrupt the workday with personal business unless an emergency or a dire social crisis is involved.

———

Although a gentleman is always careful in wording his e-mails, he is especially meticulous about doing so in work-related situations. If he feels that a situation is potentially contentious or complex, he discusses it face-to-face.

Body Work

While a gentleman always pays close attention to his personal hygiene, he may encounter coworkers who are not quite so careful when it comes to matters of cleanliness. He may find himself frequently in conversation or in collaboration with a fellow employee with chronically bad breath or unpleasant body odor. (In some cases these problems may be health related; in other cases they are the result of the coworker's failure to brush his teeth after lunch or his neglecting to take a quick shower after his noontime workout.) At the other extreme, he may be trapped in meetings with a coworker who is given to dousing himself or herself with heavy cologne or perfume.

If a gentleman is on friendly terms with his fellow employee and feels comfortable speaking frankly to him or her, he takes advantage of a private moment—when only the coworker and he are present—to say, "Ogden, you might want to think about keeping a toothbrush in your desk. It might come in handy after lunch [or after our coffee break]," or "Rick, it might be a good idea for you to make sure you have time for a shower after your workout."

He does not beat around the bush. For instance, when it comes to the overuse of cologne, which may in fact even make the gentleman physically ill, he says (once again, in private), "Marian, I think it's only right I tell you that sometimes your perfume is pretty heavy." He does not make light of the situation or risk insulting his coworker by exclaiming, "My god, Marcel, did you take a bath in that cologne?"

If he does not feel comfortable speaking directly to his fellow employee, he mentions the matter to that person's supervisor, and lets the boss handle the matter from that point forward.

A gentleman always keeps business cards in his desk and his briefcase. If a new business acquaintance offers him a card, he treats it with respect, slipping it into his pocket or his wallet. He does not leave it behind, and he does not use it to clean his fingernails.

———

A gentleman keeps his address book—whether it is on his computer or in his desk drawer—up to date.

———

A gentleman learns the names of receptionists, administrative assistants, and secretaries at the offices where he makes frequent calls. He thanks them for their assistance as often as possible.

Breaking Up

Even if a gentleman is not meticulous about how he behaves in his own kitchen, he maintains higher standards in the office break room or the communal kitchen. He never leaves his dirty coffee cup, dishes, or silverware in the sink. He does not leave his leftovers in the office refrigerator for an excessively long time. And he never assumes that he has an automatic right to sample anything left in the refrigerator by a fellow employee. At the office, as at home, a gentleman always refills the ice trays.

If fellow workers are sitting together in the break room, a gentleman always asks before joining their table. He knows that, in some cases, they may actually be conducting business or discussing matters that are not the gentleman's concern. If they tell him, "Well, right now, Gareth, we've got some business we're trying to finish up," he does not take offense.

When a gentleman changes his office address, e-mail address, or phone number, he informs his business associates as quickly as possible.

————

A gentleman shares his home phone number, personal cell phone number, or personal e-mail address only with those business associates who really need it. Except in extraordinary circumstances, he does not divulge the home phone numbers, personal cell numbers, or personal e-mail addresses of people who work with him.

Dressing Down

In some office environments, "Casual Fridays" are a standing tradition, the one day a week when the office dress code eases up and employees are permitted (and even encouraged) to dress more informally, as a means of acknowledging the onset of the impending weekend. When a gentleman starts work at a new office, however, he does not take it for granted that every week closes with a casual day. Unless he is told otherwise, he comes to work on Friday dressed precisely the way he dresses for any other work day.

Even if his office does subscribe to a "Casual Fridays" policy, a gentleman still dresses neatly and professionally. He may choose to wear chinos, a polo shirt, or a sports shirt with a blazer, and loafers. Unless, over the course of time, he observes coworkers wearing jeans, he does not even think of doing so.

If a gentleman discovers, during a large business meeting, that he needs to use the bathroom, he leaves the room quietly. He does not need to announce where he is going or when he plans to return. When he must leave a small meeting, he excuses himself, saying, "I'll be back in a few minutes."

———

A gentleman does his part to keep the men's room at his office as sanitary as possible.

———

A gentleman does not seize upon the restroom as a place to pass along office gossip. He never knows, after all, who may walk into the room, or out of a stall, at any moment.

Chapter Nine

A GENTLEMAN GETS EQUIPPED

A gentleman knows how to sew on a button. In his bathroom cabinet and in his desk at the office, he keeps a needle and thread.

———

A gentleman keeps a good quality corkscrew in his kitchen drawer.

———

A gentleman never runs out of toilet paper.

———

If a gentleman is pressed for time and if he can afford it, he has someone else clean his house for him.

A Checklist for a Gentleman's Linens

Although he may not use them himself every day, a gentleman has on hand:

- At least a half dozen heavy white cotton dinner napkins. (Even if he has dinnerware only for four, he is wise to have a couple of extra napkins on hand, in case of spills and so that he can use one to line the bread basket.)
- At least a half dozen heavy white cotton cocktail napkins.
- A couple of spare packs of heavy paper cocktail napkins.
- A half dozen heavy cotton kitchen towels. (Otherwise, he will find himself using his dinner napkins to wipe up messes in the kitchen.)

In the bathroom, in the cabinet under the sink, he keeps the following items:

- At least two good fluffy cotton towels that he does not use every day. (Even an unexpected overnight guest deserves a fresh towel.)

- At least two washcloths that match his towels.
- At least two hand towels for guests to use. (These should not be the same ones he uses every morning to wipe his face after shaving.)

A gentleman always carries a handkerchief. Because it is always clean, he readily lends it to others.

———

A gentleman always writes in either black or blue-black ink.

———

A gentleman always has a box of good-quality, heavy cardboard correspondence cards on hand for his informal correspondence–thank-you notes, sympathy notes, replies to formal invitations, even the occasional billet-doux. They may be plain, imprinted, or engraved with his name.

———

A gentleman maintains a stock of good-quality writing papers for his personal use. For most social correspondence, he uses the readily available standard-size 7¼ x 10½ inch paper known as monarch sheets.

A Checklist for a Gentleman's Glassware

Because he is likely to entertain with some frequency, and because things do get broken, a gentleman keeps a good supply of glassware. Because at least some of his guests are likely to be other gentlemen, he goes for unfussy, hard-to-break patterns that rest comfortably in the hand. On his glassware shelf he keeps:

- At least eight "old-fashioned" glasses for whiskey and other on-the-rocks drinks. (They can also be used for fruit juice at breakfast.)
- At least eight double old-fashioned glasses for mixed drinks, such as vodka and tonic. (They also serve perfectly well for soda and iced tea.)
- At least eight large multipurpose wineglasses. (The bubble shape, although intended primarily for red wine, will work for almost anything. What's more, even if a gentleman does not drink wine, they are great for desserts, like ice cream with a dribble of chocolate sauce.)
- A half dozen brandy snifters if he is the brandy-drinking sort.

———

A gentleman does not waste his money on pilsner glasses for beer. He is content to drink his beer from a can or a bottle, as long as he uses a cocktail napkin.

A Gentleman's Checklist for Dinnerware

Even if he entertains only on the rarest of occasions, a gentleman is equipped with everything necessary to set a basic dinner table. In his kitchen cabinets, he has available:

- At least four dinner plates that match. (Heavy pottery or white dishwasher-safe bistro-style plates are fine. They are also microwave safe.)
- At least four salad plates that look nice with the dinner plates. (They need not match one another, but they must look good together on the same table.)
- At least four soup bowls that complement the dinner plates. (Hearty ones, large enough for chili or beef stew, are best.)
- At least four matching cups and saucers.
- At least four coffee mugs (preferably matching, but a collection of souvenir mugs will function perfectly well).
- Flatware (probably stainless) for four, including:

- Four knives
- Four dinner forks
- Four salad forks
- Four soup spoons
- Four coffee spoons

How to Read a Newspaper

A gentleman reads a national newspaper, preferably the *New York Times*, on a regular basis. He may choose to read his newspaper online, at any time of day. But he may also cherish the tradition of holding an actual newspaper in his hands, first thing in the morning. Because a gentleman may find himself enjoying his newspaper while he is on a train, in a subway car, or in a car pool, he knows how to read his paper in the most efficient manner, without disturbing others.

1. A gentleman begins by stiffening his newspaper before him, the entire front page at his command.
2. A gentleman folds his newspaper in half vertically.

3. A gentleman folds his vertical newspaper in half again, bringing the bottom half up behind the top half.

4. Once a gentleman has finished reading the top half of his newspaper, he flips the paper over and reads the news on the bottom half. (In a newspaper with a classic layout, most of the front-page stories will "jump" to the same inside page.) He waits to read the "jumps" of the stories until he has finished reading everything of interest to him on the front page.

As a gentleman reads through his newspaper, he maintains his vertical fold, folding the bottom and top halves up and down, as need be. By doing so, he prevents the pages of his newspaper from flipping into the face of the person sitting next to him. He prevents the unnecessary rustling of newsprint, as well.

gentleman makes sure that all his erware is unchipped and clean before he puts it on the table. Even if his flatware has been through the dishwasher, he rubs it with a cloth before setting the table so that it takes on a little shine.

———

A gentleman has a rudimentary knowledge of at least one foreign language.

———

A gentleman considers it a wise investment to pay for ballroom dancing lessons.

———

A gentleman makes a will, both for his own peace of mind and out of consideration for others.

Chapter Ten

EXTREME ETIQUETTE

A Gentleman Faces the Really Big Challenges

MEETING ROYALTY

There is nothing casual about an encounter with royalty. If a gentleman is presented to the queen of England, for example, he must wait for her to initiate any conversation and he must not touch her unless she extends her hand first. (The gentleman will not be called upon to introduce himself since a member of the queen's entourage will already have informed her of his name.) He refers to her as "Your Majesty" or "Ma'am," allows her to ask all the questions, and waits for her to bring the conversation to a close.

Other royalty, including other members of the British royal family, are addressed as "Your Royal Highness" or "Ma'am" or "Sir."

If a gentleman is a citizen of the United States, he does not bow or even nod his head to another country's ruler.

If he is wearing a hat, of course, he removes it as a gesture of respect.

An Invitation to the White House

If a gentleman is invited to the White House, for any occasion, he must not refuse. Only in the case of a death in the family or a serious illness may he decline.

If the invitation is a formal one (engraved on heavy paper, complete with the presidential seal), a gentleman must respond to it formally, writing by hand. If the invitation is more casual, perhaps a telephone call from the president's secretary or an assistant to the first lady, a gentleman responds in kind. An e-mail response is not appropriate.

If the invitation is for a daytime event, such as a luncheon, a gentleman wears a dark suit. If the occasion is a dinner or some other evening event, the gentleman wears black tie. White-tie dinners at the White House have become rare in recent years. The White House invitation will make it clear if evening clothes are required.

Meeting the President

Preparing to meet the president in a receiving line, a gentleman goes ahead of the woman who is his companion. He waits for the president to initiate a handshake and any passing conversation. A gentleman refers to the president as "Sir" (or someday, as "Ma'am") or as "Mr. President" ("Madame President").

The president's spouse is referred to by his or her married name, "Mrs. Coolidge," for example, or "Mr. Coolidge."

A gentleman must arrive well ahead of time for any event at which the president will be in attendance, since protocol requires that the president must be the last person to enter the room. As long as the president is standing, everyone else in the room remains standing as well. Guests may not leave the room until after the president has departed.

How to Kiss a Lady's Hand

If he travels in Europe, a gentleman may find himself expected to kiss a lady's hand. It is not, however, the sort of thing that happens with any frequency in the United States anymore.

Nevertheless, if a woman should extend her hand to a gentleman, palm down and extended out before her so that it is clear a handshake is not what she has in mind, the gentleman simply places his lips lightly against her skin, presses her fingers for a second, and then allows her to pull her hand away. The action, of course, requires a slight bow from the waist.

An Audience with the Pope

To obtain an audience with the pope, a gentleman must have excellent connections in the Catholic Church. If the request is granted, he will receive a ticket for an audience at a specific time at the Vatican.

A gentleman wears his most businesslike, most dignified suit.

Everyone stands as the pope enters and leaves the audience chamber. The service will consist of a brief sermon by the pope followed by a blessing. Even non-Catholics are expected to kneel and stand along with the rest of the congregation. However, they need not cross themselves. If there is time, the pope may greet the visitors individually. The pope is referred to as "Your Holiness."

Meeting Other Public Figures

Whenever a gentleman is given the opportunity to meet a celebrity—from the realms of sports, politics, or the arts—he treats that person with simple respect. Fawning adulation is not necessary.

A gentleman would never intrude on a celebrity—or anyone else whom he does not know, for that matter—during an intimate dinner or a private conversation.

If the gentleman feels he must make the most of the moment, he begins by saying, "Excuse me." He may then wish to offer a compliment such as, "I loved *Tomorrow Isn't Forever*. I think it's my favorite of all your films"; but he does not seize the opportunity to say, "Why did you make a piece of trash like *Itch and Scratch*?" When his brief encounter with stardom is finished, the gentleman simply says, "Thank you for your time."

Other Forms of Address for Dignitaries

The Vice President
"Mr. (Madame) Vice President" or "Sir (Madame)"

A United States Senator
"Senator _____"

A Member of the House of Representatives
"Representative _____"

Governor of a State
"Governor _____"

An Episcopal or Roman Catholic Bishop
"Bishop _____"

A Roman Catholic Archbishop
"Your Excellency"

A Rabbi
"Rabbi _____"

A Member of the Protestant Clergy
"Mr. _____," "Mrs. _____,"
"Ms. _____," or "Dr. _____"

EXTREMELY FORMAL MOMENTS
AT THE DINNER TABLE

How to Use a Finger Bowl

If lobster or fresh fruit that must be peeled and eaten with your hands is served at a restaurant, a finger bowl may be placed on the table.

Either flowers or a slice of lemon will be floating in the bowl, so a gentleman will not make the mistake of drinking the finger-bowl water.

A gentleman dips his fingers in the finger bowl to remove sticky juices or sauces. He dries his fingertips with his napkin. A server will remove the finger bowl as soon as it has served its purpose.

How to Eat Caviar

Caviar is most often served nowadays as an hors d'oeuvre, spread on wheat crackers or spooned into hollowed-out new potatoes. It may be served as a first course, presented on a small plate along with some crusts of bread and traditional accompaniments such as grated onion, grated egg, and capers.

A gentleman remembers that caviar is salty and a little goes a long way. He uses his napkin carefully, since black fish eggs can make an ugly stain on the front of his white shirt.

How to Eat an Artichoke

Usually an entire artichoke will be on your plate. Its leaves will point upward. A gentleman pulls each leaf off, dips it in the provided sauce, and scrapes it between his teeth to remove the tender flesh. Once all the leaves are gone, a hairy little island will remain in the middle of the artichoke. This is the "choke." A gentleman uses his knife and fork to slice it away, uncovering the delicious artichoke heart underneath. He cuts the heart into bite-size pieces and dips them in the sauce before eating them.

A finger bowl may be placed on the table so that a gentleman may clean his fingers.

How to Eat Snails

If a gentleman encounters snails—or
escargot (pronounced "ess-car-go")—at
a dinner party, he will be provided with
the necessary equipment for eating them.
A special pair of tongs to grip the snail
and a small fork for pulling the meat out
of the shell will be provided. If no tongs
are provided, the gentleman must use his
fingers to hold the shell. He makes sure to
get a good grip. Otherwise, the rounded
shells may go sailing around the room.

The tiny shellfish fork is placed on the
right side of the plate, outside the knife and
spoon.

The Scoop of Sorbet

At some grand-scale banquets or formal restaurants, after the main course, a gentleman may be presented with a small scoop of citrus- or liqueur-flavored sorbet in a dish. This is not dessert. It is merely a break in the meal so that the tartness of the sorbet can clear away the heavy taste of the entrée. Sorbet is usually followed by a salad course.

A Final Word

A gentleman never makes himself the center of attention. His goal is to make life easier, not just for himself but for his friends, his acquaintances, and the world at large.

Because he is a gentleman, he does not see this as a burden. Instead, it is a challenge he faces eagerly every day.

INDEX